The Essential EHCP Guide for Parents and Carers

of related interest

The Family Experience of PDA
An Illustrated Guide to Pathological Demand Avoidance
Eliza Fricker
ISBN 978 1 78775 677 9
eISBN 978 1 78775 678 6

Can't Not Won't
A Story About a Child Who Couldn't Go to School
Eliza Fricker
ISBN 978 1 83997 520 2
eISBN 978 1 83997 521 9

Thumbsucker
An Illustrated Journey Through an Undiagnosed Autistic Childhood
Eliza Fricker
ISBN 978 1 83997 854 8
eISBN 978 1 83997 855 5

The Teens Guide to PDA
Laura Kerbey and Eliza Fricker
ISBN 978 1 80501 183 5
eISBN 978 1 80501 184 2

The ESSENTIAL EHCP GUIDE for PARENTS and CARERS

Dr Abigail Fisher

Illustrated by **Eliza Fricker**

Jessica Kingsley Publishers
London and Philadelphia

First published in Great Britain in 2026 by Jessica Kingsley Publishers
An imprint of John Murray Press

1

Copyright © Abigail Fisher and Eliza Fricker 2026

The right of Abigail Fisher and Eliza Fricker to be identified as the Author of the Work has been asserted by them in accordance with the Copyright, Designs and Patents Act 1988.

All rights reserved. No part of this publication may be reproduced, stored in a retrieval system, or transmitted, in any form or by any means without the prior written permission of the publisher, nor be otherwise circulated in any form of binding or cover other than that in which it is published and without a similar condition being imposed on the subsequent purchaser.

A CIP catalogue record for this title is available from the British Library and the Library of Congress

ISBN 978 1 80501 8 377
eISBN 978 1 80501 8 384

Printed and bound in Great Britain by Clays Ltd

Jessica Kingsley Publishers' policy is to use papers that are natural, renewable and recyclable products and made from wood grown in sustainable forests. The logging and manufacturing processes are expected to conform to the environmental regulations of the country of origin.

Jessica Kingsley Publishers
Carmelite House
50 Victoria Embankment
London EC4Y 0DZ

www.jkp.com

John Murray Press
Part of Hodder & Stoughton Ltd
An Hachette Company

The authorised representative in the EEA is Hachette Ireland, 8 Castlecourt Centre, Dublin 15, D15 XTP3, Ireland (email: info@hbgi.ie)

Contents

    Preface 7

    SEN jargon buster 10

1. What is an EHCP? 11

2. What's going on for my child? 25

3. Getting extra support without an EHCP 39

4. Preparing to request an assessment 59

5. The EHCP process 85

6. Understanding the EHCP document 113

7. Appeals and tribunals 133

8. Annual reviews and troubleshooting 159

9. Parents' experiences of the EHCP process 179

    References 206

    Useful organisations 207

Preface

Eliza and I know from our own experience how stressful the EHCP (Education, Health and Care Plan) process can be, and how hard it can be to make sense of as a parent. I am an educational psychologist, and know the process as a professional from the inside, working with schools and local authorities to support children and staff. Eliza (who is the amazing illustrator) is a parent, who has been through the process for her child, and now works with parents who are going through the process themselves.

The book starts at the very beginning, when you might be wondering what your child needs and be confused by all the new abbreviations being thrown at you. We discuss what school can do without an EHCP, and how you might decide when/if your child really needs one. We go through the process of applying for an assessment, discussing all the issues that commonly come up at this point, and explain what to expect from the local authority and during assessments with professionals. We talk you through a plan, with examples of the sort of language you can expect to see. If you disagree with the local authority, we explain the steps of what to do, and how it all works. Towards the end of the book, we talk about some of the issues that can occur after your plan is issued, and suggest ways to work through these. The final chapter includes real stories from parents about their experience in the EHCP process, and how they found the right support for their children.

We have tried to make the book accessible and easy to read. Dip in and out to the bits which are relevant to you. There's a jargon buster at the beginning because the world of special educational needs has a lot of acronyms! You will also find real-life stories, which are based on interviews with parents, and fictional stories, which are not based on any one child or parent, but are composites, made up of real things which have happened in my professional experience. At the end of each chapter, Eliza and I chat about our own experiences, and tease out the things we think are really important for you to know.

COFFEE TIME WITH ABI AND ELIZA

Abi: Hello and welcome to this book! I'm Abigail and I'm an educational psychologist and qualified teacher.
Eliza: I'm Eliza and I'm an author-illustrator.
Abi: And this is our book about the EHCP process. We thought about starting it off with a comedy flow chart – Do you want to lose your mind? So many 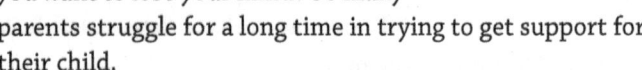 parents struggle for a long time in trying to get support for their child.
Eliza: I think if I had had something like this, which is accessible, in the beginning to read, it would have made such a difference. There's such a lack of clarity and that creates anxiety.
Abi: Can you remember the point when you didn't know what an EHCP was? You didn't know all the ins and outs?
Eliza: Well I'd heard of things like statementing, that really old language and I would associate that with children less cognitively able or physically able. I didn't realise that it might be something I might want. Or be relevant even.
Abi: Jessica Kingsley asked us to write this book because there wasn't much written to help parents going through the EHCP process. Together we have experience of the process as a professional and as a parent. I think it's fair to say we have both found there is a lot of confusion out there, and a lot of misinformation. We have tried to give you clear information so you have a solid bedrock of knowledge to start your journey.
Eliza: I think it helps to know that there is light at the end of the tunnel, there are places that work out, there are parents who get through the process and are really optimistic and love where their child is at, and they're thriving.

PREFACE

Abi: There are nine chapters here, each addressing one stage of the journey. From thinking about what your child needs, through to how to apply, what happens if you disagree with a decision, and troubleshooting issues once you have a plan. There is an overwhelming amount of information about EHCPs available, here and elsewhere, and you don't need to know it all to be successful.

We have tried to give you information to help you make your own decisions, and have included real stories so you can learn from other people's experiences. Keep your eye on the bigger picture, and what you might potentially get out of it, as you go through this bureaucratic bit. It's not you, it's the system. It's not personal.

SEN jargon buster

If you come across a word or abbreviation which is new to you, hopefully you will find a definition in this list.

Additional needs	Children with additional needs. This is the term used for children who need additional support in Scotland.
EHCP	Education, Health and Care Plan.
EHCNA	Education, Health and Care Needs Assessment.
EP	Educational psychologist.
LA	Local authority.
Needs	What your child is struggling with/their difficulties.
OT	Occupational therapist.
Provision	What extra support they need.
SEN/SEND	Special educational needs/Special educational needs and disabilities.
SENCO/SENDCO	Special educational needs coordinator/Special educational needs and disabilities coordinator. This is a person in every school whose job it is to coordinate the support for children who need something a bit different.
SEN register	Special educational needs register. This is a document which schools hold, with the names of the children who they are providing additional support for, and what their special education need is.

CHAPTER 1

WHAT IS AN EHCP?

This chapter starts from the beginning, explaining what an Education, Health and Care Plan is, what it's for, and what it can and can't do.

EHCP stands for Education, Health and Care Plan. Plans are for children and young people from birth to 25 who need something a bit different to what most children their age need. This might include specialist equipment, additional staff with specific experience or training, access to a different type of school, or other things which your child's school don't ordinarily offer to all their pupils, or can't afford without additional funding.

An EHCP brings lots of information together and makes a plan for your child's education. As part of the process, lots of different perspectives are integrated and made sense of, including assessments, professional opinions, your child's developmental history (what's happened as they've grown up), their school experiences, and your perspective. As an educational psychologist writing a report for the process, I am always thinking about what's working for your child, and what isn't.

You might hear an EHCP referred to as a 'statutory assessment', which means the final plan is legally binding. Statutory means 'written in law' and the local authority is obligated to provide what is written in the plan. This means that if it is not being provided, you can take them to court and argue your case. The local authority is responsible for providing the education that is outlined in the plan. Although the title of the plan includes health and care, in many parents' experience they are essentially education plans, as they are instigated when there is a problem identified in education, funded by education, and managed by education. You don't need an EHCP if your child has health or care needs but their education isn't affected.

Children with a really wide range of difficulties can have a plan and some children may have one from a very young age, if they have a lifelong condition like Down syndrome or complex needs which are diagnosed at birth. Most children with an EHCP will need support in more than one area – they won't just be struggling with learning, or just struggling with language. It's an umbrella process and document which covers a really wide range of situations and needs.

What is an EHCNA?

EHCNA stands for Education, Health and Care Needs Assessment. It is defined in the Children and Families Act (2014). It is the first step in the process of getting a plan. You have to apply for an assessment, rather than apply for a plan. It sounds confusing but I wouldn't worry too much about the difference between an EHCNA and an EHCP.

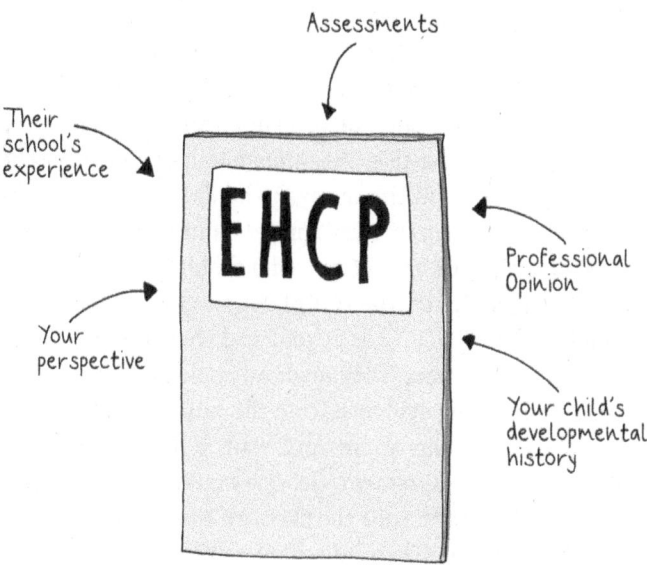

An EHCNA will identify what your child is struggling with at school and outline what might help. The parent or the school can ask the local authority to carry out an assessment. The local authority looks at the evidence and decides whether to assess a child. They make this decision based on whether your child has, or may have, SEN (special educational needs) which go beyond the support that is already available in their school or setting.

I will talk you through all of this in the rest of the book.

I'll be using stories to illustrate the process. These are based on my professional experience but they are composite stories, written to illustrate the process, and not about specific individuals. Later on you will find real-life stories from my interviews with parents about their experience in the process.

To start, here's Georgie's experience. Her daughter Marie had complex difficulties identified at birth. She went to mainstream school initially before transferring to a specialist school with more facilities on-site and a more individualised approach and curriculum.

> Marie had complex needs which had been identified at birth. She had a large health care team because of her medical needs and a diagnosis of global developmental delay and a language delay. She had had support from when she was aged one from Portage (an early years support service) and she went to a specialist nursery, where she hadn't needed an EHCP. No one mentioned it might be needed, so she started mainstream school in Reception along with everyone else. She immediately struggled as she had less support than in the nursery, she didn't understand what was going on and staff didn't understand her communication. She was scared and kept crying. She couldn't follow the phonics and writing activities the rest of the class were doing. Georgie talked to the SENDCO at school and they agreed that Marie needed more support. They made an application for an EHCNA assessment, using evidence from the nursery and from school observations. It was an anxious wait, but the local authority agreed to do the assessment. Georgie went to visit local specialist schools and identified one she liked. An educational psychologist visited Marie at home and at school, talked to staff and talked to her mum. Georgie took Marie to a speech and language therapist for an assessment of her language and communication skills. Both the professionals wrote reports which highlighted what she found difficult and they made recommendations about what she needed in her schooling. The whole process took about five months, and it wasn't easy, but eventually a final EHCP landed in Georgie's inbox, and it named the school she liked. She was extremely relieved, and Marie started there the following September.

This story illustrates how the EHCP process works in practice. Georgie and the school worked together to put in an application for a needs assessment. Marie was assessed by an educational psychologist and a speech and language therapist and they made recommendations about what she needed. These reports were put together with advice from health professionals and information from school to form the final plan for her. The EHCP plan allowed her to access a specialist school, with more support and facilities than the mainstream school. If Georgie had wanted her to remain in mainstream school, it could have provided additional adult support or resources there.

What can we do without an EHCP?
This may seem an odd place to start, but it's a good question to ask yourself. Sometimes people jump immediately to thinking they need an EHCP, and it can seem like that is the only solution, but there are often things worth exploring first. Even if you have already decided to apply for an assessment, it takes a long time for it all to happen. The process takes a minimum of 20 weeks, but it is common for it to take longer. It can take a lot longer, particularly if you end up going to mediation, have to appeal a decision or go to an SEN tribunal because you disagree with the local authority. Try not to put your

child's life on hold whilst you are waiting. Keep thinking about what could change in school right now.

> Harry was eight and was having a hard time at school. Someone told his parents that he would need a diagnosis to get extra support. They went to the GP and were put on the waiting list for an autism assessment. But they didn't realise that the waiting list was really long. In the end, it took two years for him to get to the top of the list and to be assessed. In that time, they weren't pursuing other options, as they didn't think they could access any extra support. For Harry, that meant two years in school where he was struggling more than necessary.

The EHCP process is time consuming and it's stressful. Parents say it takes a lot of energy to push the process along. It inevitably takes your time and attention away from what's going on for your child day to day in school, because you're focusing on making things better for them at the end of the process. Parents tell me that it helps to know in advance that it's going to take up time and energy so that they can plan with that knowledge, rather than ending up overwhelmed with too much going on at the same time.

If you're not sure whether you need an EHCP, it is worth making sure school are doing everything they can first. Small changes can make a really big difference and they don't have to cost money. A colleague told me how he had been able to secure time at the beginning of every day for a teenager he was working with to do their favourite thing, and that happened to be drawing horses. The student was allowed to sit in the school library and draw horses for 30 minutes first thing in the morning. For that young person, it made all the difference – and it didn't cost the school any money at all.

Getting an assessment and then getting a plan are steps along the road to meeting your child's needs, but they are part of the process and not the end of the journey. It's really important to make sure school have tried things and put in place as much as they can to support your child, because it all provides evidence for what works and what doesn't work for them.

Your child might be best supported through school-based intervention, which means an external professional works with school. This kind of lower-level support, where an educational psychologist or a specialist teacher in autism or another type of need goes into school to advise and support staff, is sometimes available via the local authority or council services, but has become much harder to access recently as resources are limited. If your goal is to improve school then it is really effective to have someone come into school, observe what's going on, and work with staff to make changes. If there are no services in your area, you could ask the SENCO to observe in the classroom. Another option to consider is therapeutic intervention. Therapies such as speech and language therapy take place over time, and help your child with specific things, such as difficulties in communication or movement. This might be available on-site as part of your child's week in a specialist school, or it might be something you are seeking in the EHCP process.

Do we really need one?

EHCPs are intended for those children who struggle most with school. This might be because they are struggling with learning, or it might be because they find things in the school environment difficult, like noise, or being around lots of people. In 2024/2025, 14.2% of children in school were identified as having SEN, whilst 5.3% of the total school population had an EHCP. This means that in order to get one, your child will need to find school more difficult than pretty much all of their classmates. If you don't think your child is one of the children who finds school hardest, then it's probably worth focusing on what school are doing first. I talk more about support in schools and understanding what your child needs in Chapter 2.

What's special about an EHCP?

- It's legally enforceable.
- Your child will be assessed by an educational psychologist.
- It identifies what your child is struggling with at school.
- It outlines how the local authority will support them.
- You will have annual reviews to update and monitor the plan.
- It might bring additional funding.
- Your child could attend a specialist setting.

What do we need to apply?

I hear from a lot of parents who are told there is no point in applying, or that their child doesn't have a high enough level of need. It can be very difficult to know what to do to best support your child in these circumstances. This story is about Joel, a child who struggled with literacy for a long time, and it wasn't clear whether he needed a plan or not.

> Joel's parents were really worried about him. He was nine and still couldn't read or write. He was very able in other ways but he was disruptive at school and getting into trouble, and he didn't want to do any of the suggested things to help learn the skills. He didn't want to do anything school-related really. They were wondering if his difficulties were severe enough for an EHCP, but school advised them that they were already offering him all the support he would get. An educational psychologist visited and watched him in class, and suggested some actions, including lifting off the pressure around reading, and focusing on things he was good at. Joel loved football so they made more time for football at school, and his parents found some Saturday morning coaching sessions. As he grew more confident in football, he felt more confident in other areas too, and gradually became more willing to engage in reading. Progress was slow, but he was willing to engage and became less disruptive.

Joel's story illustrates that some needs are not permanent, and with the right support and advice children like Joel don't need an EHCP.

WHAT IS AN EHCP?

School may be saying to you that your child doesn't have a high enough level of need to get an EHCP. Lots of parents tell me the school SENCO said 'we wouldn't get one' and 'it's not worth applying'. SENCOs have direct experience of the EHCP process in your local area so they have very useful expertise and an understanding of the process from the inside. They are often very aware of the challenges of the EHCP process, and they work within local authority policies and procedures.

Sometimes you might feel your child needs more support, but school feel they have done all they can. A parent told me school staff said they couldn't give her child ear defenders, because if they did, all the children would want them. Sometimes staff say 'it's not fair to do it just for them' or 'we can't do that for everyone'. You may have to argue your child's case, and justify why they need additional support. Schools are allowed to do things differently for individual children, because children are not all the same, and they need different things.

There are lots of 'gatekeepers' for special needs resources. These are people who have to agree to unlock the 'gate', and at each stage you have to persuade them that they should open it, to let you through to the next stage. The easiest way to get through the gate is usually through using evidence. This means concrete information and observations, often written, and often from professionals.

The first gatekeeper is the SENCO in school. Before you are even considering making an application for a needs assessment, you will be talking with school about your concerns. Most schools are able to make a wide range of small changes for your child to help school work better for them. They can change environmental aspects of the classroom, provide equipment, alter tasks and activities, and change how adults interact with them. If those changes aren't enough to help with the problems, then you might need more support than school can provide, which is when you might need an EHCP. You start this process by putting in a request for an assessment.

It is normal for the local authority to have a list of things they require a school to give evidence of before they put a request in. Sometimes local authorities stipulate rules such as 'the child must be two years behind academically to receive additional support'. Schools have to show they've been putting things in place over time, and prove that they've been spending money supporting your child. The school has to show that they're not jumping immediately to the 'emergency bell', and calling for help and extra money. It makes sense that the local authority asks for this proof of how they are supporting your child, because they need to make sure school are using their money appropriately. The local authority is protecting their resources, so they keep the additional funding for children who really are struggling the most.

This story is about Yasuda, whose needs had never been identified, but when she started secondary school it became very apparent that she needed a bit more help, and her mother asked the school to apply for an assessment. They felt they didn't have enough evidence yet, and wanted to give it more time for Yasuda to settle in, but Yasuda's mother felt she needed more support urgently, so decided to make the application herself.

> Yasuda was 11 and had moved school several times, so there had rarely been enough time for staff to notice and think about what was going on for her. Starting secondary school was a bit of a shock and things quickly became quite difficult. She immediately struggled with navigating the large building, seeing lots of teachers, and organising herself. Her mother was worried because she was falling behind, wasn't making friends, and starting to say she didn't want to go to school.

WHAT IS AN EHCP?

The school didn't think she met the criteria for an EHCP and said they wouldn't apply for a needs assessment for her. Yasuda's mum, with help from a friend who was a teacher, filled out the application herself and explained what she thought her daughter was struggling with. The local authority agreed to assess her and an educational psychologist came to visit her at school, and did some tests and talked to staff. They highlighted her difficulties with language and social communication which hadn't been recognised before. They made recommendations about what she needed, and she got an EHCP which detailed the extra things school needed to provide for her.

Yasuda's mother made the application here, because the school weren't seeing Yasuda's difficulties. An application for an EHCNA can come from the school or the parent. It is usually seen as stronger if it comes from the school. However, if you apply as a parent, you don't need to show as much evidence as the school needs to show the local authority.

Legally, you only have to show that your child might have special educational needs and that they might need additional provision. If those things are true, then according to the SEN Code of Practice (DfE & DoH, 2015), the local authority has to agree to assess your child. I worked with a parent whose SENCO told her to make the application because she knew that the application was more likely to be accepted that way. In the majority of scenarios, I think of this option as Plan B. It is always better to work with school as far as possible; in any case, the local authority will always ask school to provide evidence as part of the process.

The SEN Code of Practice

The SEN Code of Practice (DfE & DoH, 2015) is the key legal document which guides and explains the duties of schools and local authorities. It sets out what an EHCP is for and outlines the rules which local authorities must follow and use to make their decisions. It is the government guidance on the special educational needs and disability system, and it applies in England. It doesn't apply to independent schools, although children can still go to independent schools with EHCPs.

> The SEN Code of Practice says that a plan is for children with complex, long-term needs who need:
>
> - resources above those ordinarily available
> - long-term help and support from more than one agency.
>
> OR are making limited progress despite evidence of high levels of support.

How do we decide whether to apply?

Whether your child needs a plan or not is always a judgement call. It's always a balance between what the school can provide, what expertise and experience they have with your child's difficulties and how much your child is struggling, and how much energy and resources you have to put into the process.

If you think school have some more things to try, then it's worth giving it more time. If you have lost confidence in school – perhaps it feels like they don't understand what's going on, or they're not taking you seriously, or perhaps they just can't put in place what they say they're going to do – then it might be the right time to request an assessment. If there is a transition approaching, the EHCP moves with your child, so it provides a guide for the next school about what their needs are, and what provision the school needs to put in place.

When you are making the judgement call about whether to apply or not, these factors (which can be remembered with the acronym 'PHONE') are important to consider:

Proof: What evidence does school have? How long have school been providing additional support? What have they tried? Have any other professionals been involved? You might have reports from other professionals, you might have a timetable of what school are providing, you might have records of meetings with school.

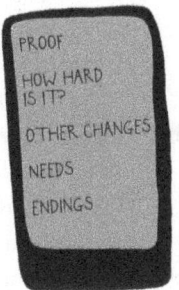

How hard is it? How difficult is it for your child? How unhappy are they? How much is the rest of their life (and yours) affected by these struggles?

Other changes: Are there any other changes you could make that would improve things for your child – at home or at school? Perhaps there are other things affecting them which are temporary and things will improve in school if they can get support with those things.

Needs: How well do you and school understand your child's needs? Do you understand what they are struggling with at school?

Endings: If there is a transition coming up – like to secondary school, or a new school, sometimes staff suggest waiting to see how it goes. I used to give this advice, but now I often suggest it is wise to get the information from the first school, which knows them well, on record.

COFFEE TIME WITH ABI AND ELIZA

Abi: It's a long-term decision and the process can take a long time.

Eliza: Parents I work with are often very focused on the day to day, because we're coping with a lot. But sometimes we need to think about the longer term, and think, is this sustainable? What is going to change going forwards? What transitions are coming up? That's a good way to think about the judgement call.

Abi: I think it's really confusing, when you're starting out looking for support, because one person says one thing, and someone else says another. The language is all new. And quite often the person in school will say you don't need one, and will try and reassure you that everything is okay as it is.

Eliza: I think it's not about looking at it in terms of what the school may be doing in terms of support or strategies that are in place. Even if they're working, it's not just about the short term, you've still got to think about the long term.

Abi: You mean because the school might not think about the long term?

Eliza: Yes, and the next place might not have what they need. So if you're in primary, you've got secondary.

Abi: So as a parent, you would suggest going for it most of the time? Quite a lot of this chapter probably comes from my local authority experience, because you have to weigh up the needs of everyone. Sometimes children don't need one, if there's only need in one area. Often, with something like dyslexia, they don't need an EHCP; schools can support that without anything extra.

Abi: I think the thing that really strikes me is you have to be very, very persistent. People are going to say you don't need one. And if you've weighed everything up and decided you do, then you have to keep going.

CHAPTER 2

WHAT'S GOING ON FOR MY CHILD?

Seeing your child through a 'deficit lens'
When your child enters the special educational needs system, it can involve a shift in thinking and the language that people use to talk about them. Parents tell me that it can feel like looking at your child through a 'deficit lens' or SEN glasses. It's the opposite of what we normally do as parents, when you see the best in your child and focus on their development and progress in relation to themselves. Professionals will compare your child with other children of the same age. It might feel like your child is being viewed as 'different' and as though there's something wrong with them. They might get a diagnosis as a way of explaining what's wrong, and as validation for the struggles.

Professionals usually need to hear from you about the most difficult times, the most challenging behaviour, or the times of most distress, and how hard it is for your family. This is a really uncomfortable time for lots of parents. It is hard to dwell on the most difficult times and having to prove how tricky things are.

The number of children diagnosed with special educational needs is increasing year on year in the UK. A parliamentary report found that in January 2024, 18% of English children were identified as having some sort of SEN (Long & Roberts, 2025). This represents a significant proportion of the school-aged population. Children are not all the same, and they don't all learn at the same rate, they don't all develop the same skills at the same time. Similarly, as adults, we don't all have the same skills, and we all have strengths and weaknesses in different areas.

Children encounter problems when their school is not able to flex and adjust to what they need. This might be for a range of reasons, and I don't mean to imply that school staff are not willing or don't understand your child. The nature of schools and age-grouped classes can mean that children are expected to be capable of particular things when they turn a certain age, and if that doesn't happen, it is seen as a problem. In the UK, five-year-olds are meant to start learning to read, and by the age of seven or eight most are expected to be fluent readers. Eleven-year-olds need to organise themselves in a large school environment, moving from classroom to classroom and remembering which books to bring each day. If they can't, then it's a problem. Some children can and do meet these expectations, but a significant proportion can't meet them. When they can't, this quickly becomes a problem for them and those around them.

Thinking about your child's needs

> Indira knew her nine-year-old son was struggling in school but she didn't really understand what his difficulties were. He didn't seem to have any friends and he seemed to find the work very hard. He never knew what he was meant to do for homework so it was hard to help. She had met with the teacher a few times and they had suggested a few things she could try at home. She wasn't sure how to go about helping him in school, or whether she should just go ahead and apply for an EHCNA.

Parents sometimes say to me that they don't know what their child needs and it is up to the professionals to decide. But parents usually know more than they think they do. Having a go at answering some of these questions might help you to articulate what you already know, and put it down clearly on paper, so it is easier to talk about with other people. It might help give you confidence in conversations with school and other professionals. It might help you think about what would help your child at school.

The activities are not essential. If you didn't like school yourself and don't really want to think about what it's like, don't put yourself through it. If you don't have time to do any of them, it's okay.

Thinking about what your child is finding hard

Starting to really think about what your child struggles with can be upsetting. I would recommend setting aside some time when you won't be disturbed, and can allow yourself to think properly. Plan for some time afterwards as well if you can, to do something for yourself.

Even if your child already has a diagnosis of a neurodevelopmental disorder, I would still recommend doing this. Every child is different, and what a diagnosis actually means for them will be individual. Try and start from what your child is like and what you know about them based on your experiences with them.

Don't assume you already know what the problem is, and don't assume you know what the solution is. There are usually lots of possible routes to take which would help.

ACTIVITY 1: Questions to ask yourself

Start by trying to make a list of what they find difficult. These questions might be a helpful place to start.

- When are the most difficult times?
- What are you most concerned about?
- What are school most concerned about?
- Do they find it hard to change from one activity to another?
- Are they struggling with writing, or using cutlery/scissors?
- Can they ride a bike, hop, balance?
- Do they seem to be constantly disagreeing with their peers?
- Do they find it hard to put their thoughts into words?
- Do they find it hard to sit still or concentrate?
- Are they worried about everything?
- Do they dislike loud noises or big groups of people?
- Do they find it hard to change plans or their routine?
- Do they find it hard to manage their emotions?
- Do they find it hard to make mistakes, perhaps they are quite perfectionist?
- Are they independent in a way that is appropriate for their age? Think about dressing, eating, toileting, using money, independent travel.
- Is it hard for them to follow instructions, or complete tasks?
- Do they take the rules or what others say very literally?

WHAT'S GOING ON FOR MY CHILD?

In trying to work out your child's needs, you know more than you think you do. It's helpful, though sometimes painful, to be explicit about what they can't do.

> Charlie sat down with her friend Helen to go through the questions and think about her daughter Ellie who is in Year 8. They left out the ones which didn't seem relevant to them and added in a few extra things they thought of. Helen helped Charlie to write down the key points.
> This is what she wrote:
>
> - Most difficult times – Going to school in the mornings, Sunday evenings. Homework – takes forever and never clear what to do.
> - I am concerned about – Getting her to school.
> - School are concerned about – She's not making progress and getting further behind.
> - Finds writing hard. Can't use cutlery very well. Can ride a bike.
> - She is really anxious at school and constantly worried.
> - Can only sit for a short period before she is in pain. At home she moves a lot, and fidgets constantly.
> - Fine with most transitions and changes to plans.
> - Independent in most things as expected.
> - Writing is painful and she can't sit upright very well. Had OT support at primary school.
> - Doesn't take things literally but can't understand long instructions – she needs you to break them up for her.
> - Struggles to concentrate and pay attention for long periods – seems to check out.
> - Has some friends.

ACTIVITY 2: Comparison

Bring to mind a child, of a similar age to your child, who you know well. It could be a sibling, a cousin, or a friend. Take some time and sit down and really think through the things your child can't do yet which other children close to them in age are able to. Perhaps you can't leave your child at a friend's house, maybe they can't go to the shop independently, perhaps they have meltdowns just at the thought of going into town. Maybe they won't have anything to do with a book or don't appear to recognise their name.

> Charlie compared her daughter Ellie to her niece, Becky, who is the same age. She really didn't want to do this activity, because it felt really negative, but they decided to try it. This is what Helen wrote down.
>
> - Becky goes to youth club and tennis – Ellie has tried them but found youth club overwhelming, and she struggles with the motor control for tennis.
> - Becky has sleepovers and meets her friends in town at the weekend to go shopping. Ellie won't go to a sleepover and doesn't want to go to town on her own. She says she's scared.
> - Becky is going on the language exchange next year – Ellie hates French so says she doesn't want to go.
> - Becky has read whole series of books and apparently loves reading. Ellie finds reading such hard work she avoids it at all costs.
> - Becky loves writing stories and drawing comics in her spare time. Ellie hates writing because it hurts her.

Charlie hadn't wanted to do this activity, but she actually found it quite cathartic. It was helpful to see it all written down, and it highlighted to her that she needed to try and develop Ellie's independence, and find ways to help her take some steps outside the home. Her friend encouraged her to take the list to school as well, so she did, although she was very anxious about what they might say. Having a written list provided a useful place to start for the meeting. School hadn't realised that Ellie found writing painful – they just thought she was very slow at writing. The first thing they did was give her a laptop and some teaching about how to use it, which Ellie loved. She started using the text-to-speech when she had lots of reading to do for homework, and this really sped her up. She started to feel more confident.

ACTIVITY 3: Visualise your child's day

Another useful place to start is by visualising your child's day, and thinking through the bits that they find difficult, the 'crunch' points. You might want to do this twice, once to show what it's like on a bad day, the other for a good day. Go through and write down what you know about the times which are difficult. For example:

- Getting up – Is always tired as finds it hard to fall/stay asleep. Won't eat anything in the morning. Will only wear one particular top and leggings.
- Going into school – Hates crowds so they never want to walk into school.
- Break time – Always seems to be on their own.
- Science lessons – Is really anxious about science lessons and cries about science tests. Not sure teacher is aware.
- Lunchtime – They say they're bored at lunchtime and don't have anyone to hang out with.

You can use what you know about them from home to help you with what they might be struggling with in school. If you know that they hate large groups and loud noises, and they also hate walking into school, then make the connection, that's probably why. If they find it really hard to sit still or wait when they're hungry, and can be difficult to manage at those times, then note it down as an issue in that half hour before lunch. If the unstructured times like lunchtime are really hard for them, and they are often alone in the playground, note it down. If there isn't a lot in their books, and they never seem to start tasks, and struggle to finish tasks, note it down.

You might have bits of information from school reports, or from conversations with school staff, or your child, that will help you. So gradually you build up a picture in front of you of when the challenges happen.

This section has brought up a lot of things to think about. It may have challenged how you think about your child and brought issues to the fore which you haven't thought about before. Take your time, and come back to it another time. Discuss it with someone.

> Alice is a parent of two children with SEN. This is her advice for someone at the beginning of the EHCP process.
>
>> Don't beat yourself up for what you don't know yet, but take the time to learn and ask yourself, does this fit with my child? Is this relevant? Is this respectful of my child? It isn't about being an obstructive parent, it's about advocating for your child's needs. It takes a while to build your own knowledge base. You have to acknowledge that you do things with the best of intentions and you can't punish yourself for the things you didn't know at the time. If I'd known, I'd have challenged more from the start.

What are special educational needs?
What is your child struggling with?

The SEN Code of Practice (DfE & DoH, 2015) classifies children's differences into four different areas of need. Your child will be identified as belonging to one of these categories, according to which are their most pressing needs. Most children who need an EHCP have difficulties in more than one area.

Cognition and learning

Cognition means thinking and thought. Needs in this area are those related to thinking and learning. Some cognitive needs are easier to identify and are often identified early – like a significant learning difficulty which affects a child from a young age, or when they find reading or maths harder than others. Other difficulties, like finding understanding and processing information harder, or struggling to organise thoughts in order to write them down, can be more difficult to spot. Psychological factors will also affect how they approach learning in the classroom, like how confident they feel, whether they feel able to make mistakes, and the ability to tolerate frustration. As they get older, skills such as the ability to plan and prioritise, manage time, and maintain focus on their goals may become more important.

Your child might learn at a slower pace to others in the class, and need more repetition. They might be someone who needs to learn by 'doing' and being able to manipulate objects, or need things to be presented visually in order to fully understand them. They might have difficulty in organising their thoughts, or remembering things. This category includes specific learning difficulties which affect certain areas of the curriculum such as dyslexia and dyscalculia.

Communication and interaction

Your child's ability to use and understand language affects their learning, behaviour, relationships, and emotional development. These needs will change over time. Autistic spectrum disorder is the most common need identified in EHC plans in England. For those receiving SEN support in schools, the most common need is speech, language, and communication. The sorts of difficulties you might see are difficulties with speech (articulation, fluency etc.), difficulties with language (understanding and talking), and/or differences in communication (how we relate to each other). Your child might not have difficulties in all these areas. Difficulties in expressing yourself and making yourself understood can quickly lead to frustration and isolation, and can lead to children being seen as difficult in school and finding it hard to build relationships with their peers and adults.

Speech, language, and communication needs include differences in how children interact. Some children's social interactions are different to the average for their peer group. They may dislike large groups, or they may find reciprocal relationships challenging. They may still prefer to play like a younger child. They may find it harder than their peers to understand things like the concept that other people have thoughts and feelings, or that rules are sometimes flexible and not followed literally. Social differences can particularly be difficult in unstructured situations such as the playground.

Children with autism have differences in their:

- social understanding, communication, and interaction
- sensory processing and integration
- flexible thinking, information processing, and understanding (Autism Education Trust, n.d.).

Social, emotional, and mental health

If your child is struggling emotionally, you will likely notice it in their behaviour, even if they are unable to talk about it. They might become withdrawn or isolated, or they might behave in challenging ways, such as running out of the classroom, refusing to go to school, or hurting others. They might be getting into more conflict with teachers or peers. When a child is behaving in challenging ways it is important to consider if there are any underlying difficulties related to learning, language, communication, or social interaction which haven't yet been understood.

Social, emotional, and mental health needs impact children's learning and relationships. These needs change over time and fluctuate in their severity and intensity, and may be different according to the context and the environment. Children may struggle to understand and regulate their emotions, or may struggle with peer relationships. Difficulties with mood (anxiety or depression), self-harm, eating disorders, or substance abuse might all require support in school.

Sensory and/or physical

If your child has a physical disability or impairment to their hearing or vision, this category encompasses those needs. Children might need specialist equipment so they can access and function within the classroom, or they might need access to a specialist setting with physiotherapy or occupational therapy. Staff might need additional training, or they might need some input from a teacher who has special training and can support the staff who work with the child every day.

This area also includes sensory processing which affects how we integrate information that comes in from our senses, such as noise, lights, and sound. When children struggle with sensory processing it affects how they behave, and how they feel. In a noisy environment it might be hard to tune things out, or it might be so overstimulating they can't stay calm. It is a really wide range of differences and can make the classroom environment very difficult for some children.

They may experience noises as too loud, lights as too bright, smells as too intense. Children with these differences may put their hands over their ears or may complain that the dining hall smells disgusting. They may avoid the school toilets altogether. They may find wearing school uniform distressing as the texture hurts their skin.

Things people might be saying

When children struggle in school, people say all sorts of things about them; you might be thinking them too. They might be called disruptive or naughty, they might be seen as stubborn or resistant. Perhaps they're lazy or difficult. This isn't healthy for you, or them.

Your child might also have some medical diagnoses, which are another way to explain their behaviour. Sometimes getting a diagnosis feels like a relief, and it helps take the blame off the child or you as a parent. Diagnoses are labels we use to help us understand what's going on. They rarely capture the full picture and they don't tell us what a child needs. Diagnoses cover a wide range of differences and the medical term itself may not tell you very much about your child individually.

To help a teacher understand what they actually need to do to support your individual child, a description of each difficulty is usually most helpful. The exercises in this chapter are all about clarifying what your child is struggling with, connecting this with what might be happening in school, and articulating this. If you're not able to do any of these exercises, it is okay.

> Howie is in Year 5. School has never been his favourite place, but it was okay until this year. Since making the transition to Year 5, it all seems to have gotten worse. His mother is finding him very challenging and defiant at home, and his teacher says he is disruptive and doesn't apply himself. She said he is constantly arguing with his peers and doesn't have any friends. Sometimes school say it must be his hormones and it will resolve over time. They've suggested she goes on their parenting course. He is on a waiting list for various assessments, but it might take a long time. His mother sat down with the school SENCO and they thought about when the problems were happening, and wrote a list of the things that he finds difficult.
>
> - Finds transitions difficult.
> - Finds unstructured times difficult.
> - Doesn't start tasks independently.
> - Is reading below his age ability.
> - Writing is painful and very slow.
> - Finds peer relationships difficult.
> - Finds stopping favoured activities hard.
> - Finds it very hard to fall asleep.

COFFEE TIME WITH ABI AND ELIZA

Abi: When I worked as an educational psychologist for the local authority, I didn't really know much about the process from the parent's perspective. I always knew it was quite hard to read the reports as a parent, because they highlight the worse things. They are

all about the struggles. But quite how hard that is I maybe hadn't realised until I became a parent and had to go to some intimidating meetings. You don't usually share the most difficult times at home with other people.

Eliza: I think you're often quite ill-prepared as a parent to do that bit. I remember having that meeting with the educational psychologist and the SENCO and feeling quite overwhelmed after it because I don't think I had had all the cards laid out quite like that before. I didn't know that was part of the process. I think being prepared for that and knowing that we're not here to write some kind of affirmative thing is helpful.

Abi: This is a meeting where we are going to talk about the hard things. And there is a strengths section of the EHCP, but the reality is that it's the hard things that are what makes you qualify for an EHCP.

Eliza: I think that's an important part, to be prepared for what is going to come up. It's another aspect of the process you're not often prepared for, and not being prepared is where the shock comes in and you can feel awful. It packs a punch. Ultimately, it's not a nice thing to read.

Abi: You have to spell out what's really different about them at this point in time in their development in order to get the extra support, and that is cruel, but you have to do it. I used to get told off for mine being too positive because they would say, 'We can't see what the problem is', because I wrote it in such an affirmative way.

CHAPTER 3

GETTING EXTRA SUPPORT WITHOUT AN EHCP

For some children it's clear from birth or when they are very young that they will need additional support and services for their education. Other children are fine at home, and fine at nursery, but encounter problems at school or as they get older. Sometimes children make it all the way to secondary school before they need extra help.

So if you're deciding to wait to apply for an EHCP, or if you're not sure if you need one, a helpful place to start is thinking about what we can do without one. Even if this is definitely the road you are going down, I would keep thinking about what is changing for your child on the ground. What could happen now, whilst we're waiting for a needs assessment?

What can I expect from school?

If your child is in a mainstream primary or secondary school, but doesn't have an EHCP, you will likely have encountered the term 'reasonable adjustments'. This comes from the Equality Act (2010), which says that schools are required to make 'reasonable adjustments' so that all children can access their facilities and services. There is no definition of what reasonable adjustments are, and it is up to each school to decide how much they can adjust to each child. They might say yes or no based on factors such as finance, whether they think it will be effective or not, whether it's practical, and if it will affect other pupils adversely or cause health and safety issues.

Schools are allowed to say no to doing things, and they are allowed to say they can't cater to a particular need because it will affect the education of other children. The local authority has a legal duty to provide an education for every child – but there are lots of schools under their jurisdiction. Each individual school has the right to say they are unable to do certain things. Schools make different decisions based on their funding and experience, and on the views and ethos of their leadership.

The steps of support

This section will explain how some of the school systems in relation to SEN work. It will help you think about what stage your child is at, and what school are providing for them.

Most children with special educational needs will not need an EHCP. Support should be offered to them progressively, depending on what they need. This starts with support and adjustments in the classroom, and progresses to more individualised and intensive support.

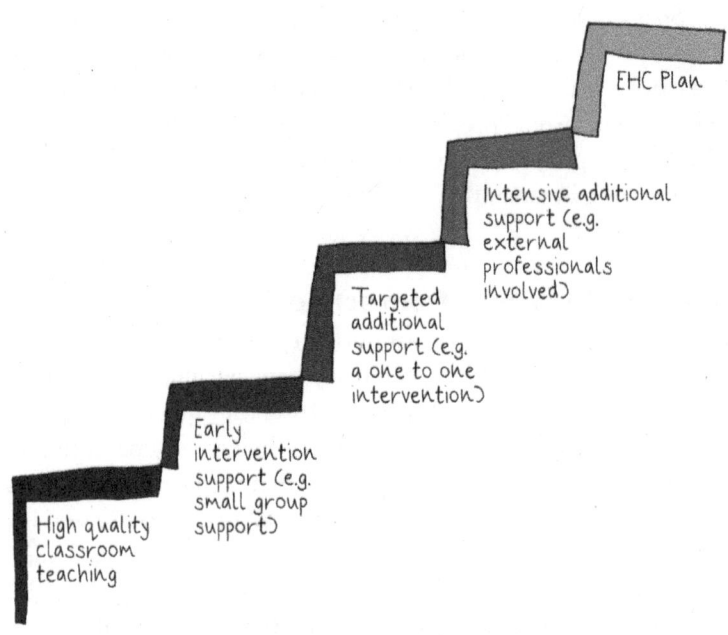

GETTING EXTRA SUPPORT WITHOUT AN EHCP

This is a diagram of how support progresses in school. As you go up the steps, there is an increasing level of support and more people become involved, giving advice or individual or group support.

Stage 1 is great classroom teaching. A good teacher will often be doing a lot to adapt to each individual in their classroom without even realising it. Sometimes you only realise how much the last teacher was doing, when the next one doesn't do those things automatically. It is very common in secondary schools for some lessons to be fine, whilst others are very problematic, because of the relationship with the teacher. Sometimes children start a new school year and it all falls apart. It's often because their last teacher understood them well and was doing a lot of invisible adjustments.

Stage 2 is called early intervention support. This might involve small groups in class, or individual support from the classroom teaching assistant, such as additional reading, or a focus on fine motor skills.

Stage 3 is targeted additional support. Your child might get daily one-to-one reading outside the classroom, or if they are older perhaps access to the SEN hub for specific lessons. The school SENCO is now involved, and they are considering putting your child on the SEN register. This is a register of all the children with SEN needs in the school. At this stage records of meetings start to be kept, as this might be needed as evidence for the EHCP process.

Stage 4 is intensive additional support. External professionals would now be involved and offering recommendations about what might help.

Stage 5 is the highest level of support and by now a considerable bank of evidence should have been brought together. If the earlier stages haven't been enough to support your child and improve things, then you would apply for an EHCNA assessment.

Although I have outlined these steps, and emphasised the need to gather evidence, it doesn't always happen like this. Sometimes there is a sudden crisis, or a rapid escalation in challenging behaviour, or your child moves school and the new staff apply for an EHCP immediately. There are circumstances when a quick application is needed and local authorities will look at the individual circumstances for each child.

Useful questions:

- What additional support is your child getting?
- Is it small group or one-to-one? Is it every day or every week?
- Is it making a difference? How do you know?
- What strategies are being used at the moment?
- Do they have time out of the classroom?
- Have they had any involvement from external professionals?
- Are they calm and happy both at school and at home?
- Are they making progress? Are you happy with their progress?
- Have you had any conversations about the next step, if it's needed?

Getting the right support in place is a process of learning and it takes time. As you go through this process, everyone involved should be developing a better understanding of your child's needs. If it is going well, you are developing a joint understanding of what the problems are. School staff may develop their skills, you might share information from home, there might be some new insight from a professional report, which all come together to create a holistic understanding of your child's difficulties, and a range of solutions to try.

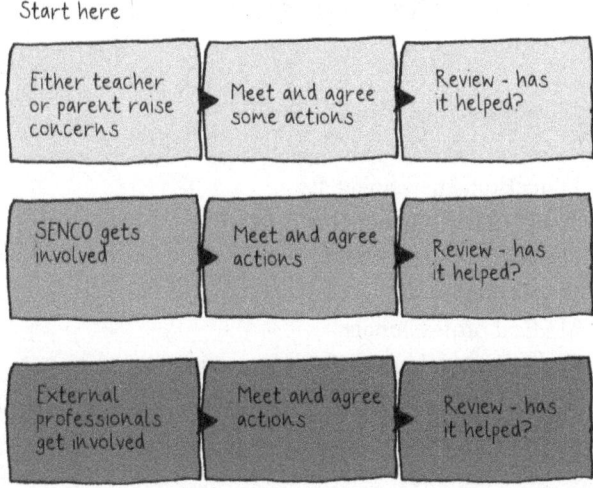

This diagram illustrates how the support process might work in school. You would initially raise concerns and meet with the teacher. At that meeting you clarify what the problem is and agree some changes. You agree to check in again to see if things have improved. You might loop round this level for a while, or this might be sufficient to address the issue. If either you or the teacher decides more help is needed, you can involve the SENCO. They might advise the teacher, conduct some observation in the classroom, or do some assessments with your child. You might all meet to agree actions, or the teacher might put things into practice and update you later.

Getting another perspective

Another perspective can be invaluable in helping the school understand your child's needs. This could be from an external professional coming into school, such as an educational psychologist or a behaviour/autism consultant. This type of lower level support has become harder to access in recent years. Within school, someone such as the SENCO could observe in the classroom or playground to try and gather more information about what's going on. Another perspective can illuminate your child's needs, can help develop staff skills, and also help you to be heard. Sometimes parents go and talk to their GP and share their concerns, and the GP can write a letter which you might share with school. This can help if you don't feel like school understand your perspective.

> Who are the external professionals?
>
> - Educational psychologists
> - Speech and language therapists
> - Occupational therapists
> - Physiotherapists
> - Medical professionals
> - Specialist teachers in literacy or numeracy
> - Autism service teachers with additional training and expertise
> - Behavioural support services
> - Teachers from specialist schools who have expertise in different ways of learning and teaching
> - Specialist support services for visual or hearing needs, or physical disabilities

A key point to realise about making adjustments is that some changes are more expensive or more difficult than others.

Changes which are more difficult:

- Things that will be just for your child – e.g. significantly slowing the pace of teaching or having an individual timetable
- One-to-one staff member time
- Large amounts of time outside the classroom
- Provision on another site, e.g. half-day at a therapy farm, afternoon at a forest school

Changes which are easier:

- Things which the whole class can join in with, e.g. short movement session every morning
- Things which staff can do in a normal day – checking in, adapting instructions, adapting tasks, writing in a home-school communication book
- Things which are already happening in school, e.g. additional reading group, lunch clubs, a quiet place to eat

It is important to remember that small changes can make a big difference. What appears to be an insignificant thing, like being able to wear a different fabric to the standard uniform, can mean a child is able to cope at school. Being able to wear comfortable clothing means overall stress levels from other things throughout the day are manageable. Stress is cumulative.

Making reasonable adjustments

Schools are not all the same. Sometimes parents are told that they are, and that if a child struggles in one, they will struggle in another. In my experience this isn't true. The expertise and experience in schools varies massively, and will vary in one school over time as staff leave, start, and develop their skills. The flexibility and ability of schools to adapt to individual children varies considerably. Some schools are better at adapting and meeting individual needs than others.

Some schools sell themselves on their flexibility and adaptability, and their overriding priority is to cater for each child's individuality. That is their mission, and they will do anything in support of it. Some schools take a one-size-fits-all approach, and they usually sell themselves on that too. They expect children to conform to their expectations.

If your child needs a lot of flexibility, and they're in a school which expects children to fit into their expectations, it might not be possible to change their approach. When you are choosing a school, tailor your choice to what your child needs.

Mainstream primary schools

Primary schools are typically more nurturing than secondary schools and they often see children's social and emotional development as an important part of their work. They are smaller communities with fewer staff, and it is often easier to make changes and try different things. They may have a part-time SENCO, or one who is a full-time teacher, so it can be hard to meet with staff who are in the classroom for much of the time. However, as only one staff member, the child's teacher, is responsible for what happens, it is often simpler, as fewer people are involved. They may have specially trained teaching assistants, or staff who have expertise in working with particular types of need.

This is a story about making reasonable adjustments for Tom, in Year 3:

> Tom had just made the transition to Year 3 and he had started not wanting to go to school. At home he was having meltdowns and was really distressed. His parents felt that all the changes in Year 3 were part of it, but were scared about asking for help because they weren't sure school would see it that way. They didn't know if they would be able to do anything to help – maybe Tom just had to adjust to the new expectations as he was getting older. They decided they had to try and were pleasantly surprised.
>
> School had experienced this problem before, as the transition had been challenging for some other children as well. So they understood the problem and suggested some adjustments.

They reinstated afternoon play for Tom, which usually stopped in Year 3. They gave him a box of fidget toys he could use in the classroom and access whenever he wanted. They also made sure he got a movement break every 30 minutes – sometimes it was an errand, sometimes a different kind of activity or something on the carpet. They were small adjustments which didn't cost any money, but Tom was happy to go to school again and calmer at home. He didn't need an EHCP.

Things which mainstream primary schools can do to help, which don't usually require an EHCP:

	Lower primary children	**Upper primary children**
Problems with learning	Spend more time in a play-based environment (e.g. accessing the Reception classroom)	Small group intervention for literacy or numeracy
	Activities which don't involve having to record/write information	Using concrete materials in maths, e.g. base 10, unifix
	Use a multi-sensory approach to learning, e.g. using resources which children can touch and interact with, making more allowance for movement during learning activities	Using talking activities before writing
		Learning activities which involve movement
		Differentiated tasks (tasks with different levels of difficulty)
		Reduce writing by printing out anything that needs to be copied
	Targeted small group activities, e.g. if not yet ready for writing, using a sand tray or foam for letter writing	Reduced or no homework demands
		Reduced or no testing requirements
		Offer a range of ways to access information and learn new concepts, e.g. YouTube videos, books, games
	Writing and number supports, e.g. number lines, high frequency word lists	Learning mentor sessions to help with organising and planning
		Instructions given one-to-one and broken down
		Additional movement breaks, e.g. running an errand, taking a message, or walking round school for five minutes

cont.

	Lower primary children	**Upper primary children**
Problems with friends	Lunchtime buddies Friendship bench Whole class activities about friendships/feelings Allow them to spend time with a sibling in another class Adult-led games at lunchtime/break time	Small group activities with adult support Tools such as comic strip conversations, social stories, to help children understand social relationships School counsellor or ELSA (emotional literacy) support
Problems with the school environment	Lunch in a quieter environment, e.g. small group in a classroom Break time inside Children can be dropped off a little earlier to avoid the rush Access to a quieter area, e.g. a sensory room/peace room	A quiet, distraction-free space to work in Go in/out quieter entrance or slightly early/late Different arrangements during assemblies, e.g. doing a preferred activity during this time Indoor or structured lunch and break options, e.g. Lego club, music club, Minecraft club

Secondary schools

Secondary schools usually have a full-time, non-teaching SENCO. They sometimes have an SEN hub, and some have specially trained teaching assistants, who will have more experience with children who need something a bit different. They may have a specialist resource base for a particular type of need, such as autism. There may be a higher level of expertise and experience in the staff team as a whole, but not necessarily amongst all staff.

Teachers who are trained as subject specialists may not have had much input around special educational needs and how to adapt their style and teaching. It can be harder to get a consistent approach in a secondary school, as young people encounter many different staff during the average day.

Transition to secondary school is often a challenging time and the cause of much worry for parents. The move from primary to secondary involves a lot of changes, and what is expected of children increases considerably. The most effective secondary schools will liaise with primary schools, so they know the needs of the children who are coming, and put things in place ready for them. There may be support already set up, such as a smaller, specialist Year 7 catch-up group, for those who need to catch up with their literacy skills before they are ready for the Year 7 curriculum. Schools sometimes use documents such as a 'pupil passport' to provide a quick way for staff to communicate key information.

Some young people don't need any additional support in primary, but struggle with the increased demands of secondary, finding managing multiple teachers, functioning in a larger, noisier environment, and organising themselves difficult. The pressure on young people also increases as they get older, with an increased focus on exams, tests, and GCSEs. This can cause anxiety and distress.

This story is about Kelly, who decided to choose a secondary school for her son based on his needs, rather than choosing the school which appeared to be the better choice.

> Kelly was choosing a secondary school for her son, Jack. Jack had thrived in his small primary school where his teachers knew him well, but she knew he struggled to organise himself, and

didn't like busy, noisy environments. The most popular local choice for secondary had an outstanding OFSTED and was academically high achieving, with ten classes of children per year. It was spread across several very large buildings. It also had some behaviour policies she didn't like, such as requiring children to be silent in the corridors. Her neighbour's kids were very happy there but she was worried Jack would find it overwhelming and might get lost. She went to look at the other secondary school in the area, which had less good results, and was a bit further away, but she immediately felt more at ease there, and could imagine Jack fitting in.

Kelly chose the school which she felt would suit her son better, rather than the one which seemed on the outside to be the best choice. She decided that for Jack with sensory needs, he would learn better and be happier at the smaller school which was quieter and easier to navigate, than the outstanding local secondary school.

Ways mainstream secondary schools can support pupils:

	Ideas for secondary aged pupils
Problems with the school environment	• Access to an SEN hub or designated space where there is additional support • Quiet, distraction-free space to work in, e.g. library • Go in and out of a quieter entrance, move around school at quiet times (e.g. five minutes early) • Use ear defenders • Different lunchtime and break time arrangements • Smaller group sizes • Different arrangements during assemblies and other large group events • Additional movement breaks, e.g. running an errand, taking a message, or walking round school for five minutes • Time out of classroom to do a preferred activity

GETTING EXTRA SUPPORT WITHOUT AN EHCP

Problems with learning	• Make sure staff understand their needs and how to adapt their teaching, language, and expectations • Additional support in lessons • Learning mentor sessions to help with organising and planning • Differentiated tasks (tasks with different levels of difficulty) • Print out lesson objectives to reduce writing load • Allow a young person to drop a less favoured subject to give more time for others • Support in note taking • Reduced or no homework demands • Reduced or no testing requirements • A range of ways to access information and learn new concepts, e.g. YouTube videos, books, games • Access to the library to complete tasks • Access to concrete materials to support maths and literacy
Support with relationships	• Make sure staff understand their needs and how to adapt their teaching, language, and expectations • Structured activities or places to go during unstructured times (i.e. lunchtime and break time) • PSHE input on friendships • Small group support during the week • Counselling or ELSA (emotional literacy) support • Lunchtime club which is set up around something they enjoy • Mentor sessions to discuss social and peer-related issues

Things school can do at SEN support level:

- Think about your child as an individual
- Meet with you regularly about the problems
- Do some assessments and gather information from staff
- Make plans and agree actions which are specifically for your child
- Provide some additional support in a small group
- Offer flexibility over start/finish times and timetable
- Involve other professionals for their advice and recommendations, e.g. an educational psychologist or speech and language therapist

Things you can expect a school SENCO to do:

- Observe in the classroom
- Advise the teacher
- One-off assessments with your child
- Meet with you
- Keep records of meetings and observations, write a report if necessary
- Put your child on the SEN register if required
- Involve external professionals as appropriate

Jade's son had involvement from the learning disability team, and when he started having problems in his specialist school, they were able to go in and observe him.

> There were some changes at school and they started going off-site more. He just could not cope with all of the moving

> about and going on a bus. We saw the behaviour at home just plummet and the school referred us to the LD team. It was framed very much as it's a parental problem. They can't cope with them at home. He's fine at school. Our learning disability nurse was lovely. She went in and observed him. She sent us her observation and I sent it back and said, this is the wrong child. It was heartbreaking. He was a completely different child at school. At school he was quiet, withdrawn, didn't say anything — they had to do 'hand over hand' all of the time, and they had just assumed that that was his learning disability.

The observation highlighted how differently he was behaving and functioning at home and school. This gave Jade information and evidence to start conversations with school about how they were managing him.

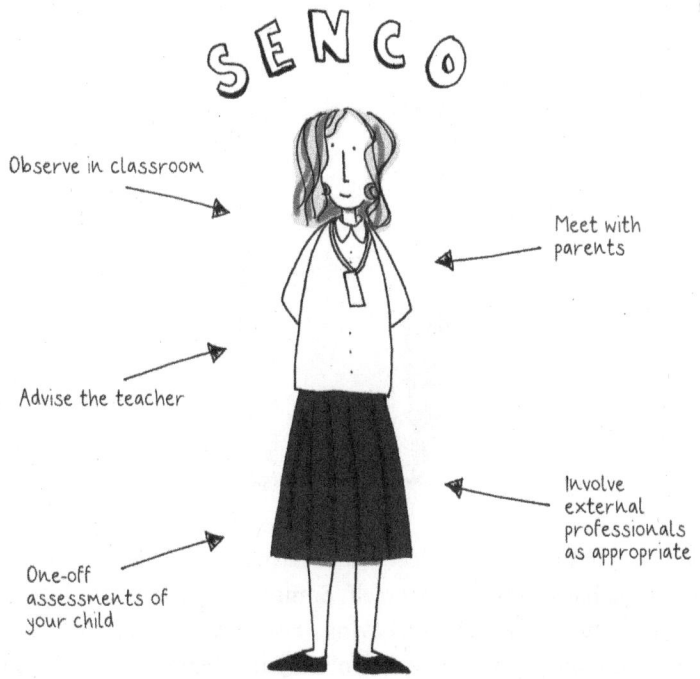

Meetings with school

There is an inherent power differential when schools work with families, and it's visible everywhere you look. In meetings and reports parents are often referred to by their first name, or even by their roles 'Mum' and 'Dad'. You might not understand the language or the acronyms they are using but it's hard to ask them to explain. Many parents say that they start to feel like children again in the school context, with teachers 'telling them off' if their child doesn't do their homework or isn't making it to school on time.

Parents often say they don't feel like they have meaningful input in meetings or when deciding actions – their role was to agree with school requirements, not to question. Parents often report feeling blamed and dismissed and that they can't win. Parents and professionals can have very different experiences of the same meetings. School staff may think a plan or contract has been mutually agreed, whilst parents feel that they have had no choice.

Meetings with school can feel intimidating – sometimes it can feel like going back to school yourself. Sometimes parents feel blamed for the problems their child is having. It can feel hard to say what you think if it is different to what school staff are saying. It can feel really hard to discuss the problems your child is having, and sometimes school staff might put things in a way which is upsetting.

> Things to try in meetings:
>
> - Write things down if you are worried about not being heard, forgetting what to say, or saying it incorrectly.
> - Take notes during the meeting – it is often hard to remember everything that was said.
> - Take another adult for support.
> - Practice saying difficult things in advance.
> - Ask people who cannot come to contribute by writing something.
> - Write down questions as they come to you when the meeting is coming up – it's hard to remember them at the right moment!

Problem corner
Things aren't getting better

I worked with Priya, a parent who first raised concerns about her 11-year-old daughter struggling at school a year ago. Priya has met with her head of year three or four times over that time, but nothing has happened. There isn't a plan and she isn't aware that they have agreed to put anything in place. School have been listening to her concerns, but nothing seems to have happened. It's really easy to spend a lot of time talking about what the problems are without agreeing any actions to help.

Things which might help

- Have you had a review meeting?
- If there were actions agreed, were people allocated responsibility to do it?

- Use regular informal check-ins – ask questions of the teacher when you see them, send a quick message to ask how things are going.

If really tricky things have happened, you can spend a lot of time talking about those, arguing about how they were handled, wanting staff to accept they were wrong – but it doesn't change what's going to happen next. It can help to narrow the focus of a meeting – decide on one thing to work on. It might feel hard to say, but anyone can help focus a meeting, by asking questions which change the direction of the conversation. It's okay to bring up things which are worrying you, and you feel need talking about, even if the staff don't raise the issue.

Useful questions for meetings

- Could we focus on X today?
- So what have we agreed to try? (If you're not sure, it's fine to check.)
- Could we set a date to come back to see if it has helped?
- Who is going to do that?
- Could we talk about X? I'm worried that...

COFFEE TIME WITH ABI AND ELIZA

Eliza: When I was starting off getting support in school it felt like it was lots of meetings, but I didn't feel like it was actually going anywhere. It felt very cloudy and confusing.

Abi: I was a teacher first, then an educational psychologist (EP), and now a parent. I never realised when I was the professional working with parents how hard it is to ask for help from school – because you don't know what you're going to get from them. You don't know whether they're going to blame you, or say unhelpful things that might make it worse.

You don't know what you want or what's possible, but you know something needs to change.

Eliza: I don't think I knew what I wanted to happen. I was just having meetings. I didn't know what I wanted. I think I was going to those meetings just to share that things were very problematic. So going to the meeting to talk about the problem, but not getting anywhere in terms of doing anything that would change it.

I think the bit about descriptive terms is really helpful because it breaks it down, the different ways that you can think about your child's difficulties. I think the descriptive terms are worth their weight in gold. That's the element that would have been missing for myself and maybe a lot of other families. We might have the medical ones, or what other people are saying, but the descriptive ones are what you need really. If I had had those descriptive terms to feed to those professionals, that might've created a different outcome because we've all got something to work from.

It also helps with how you might talk to your child about it. How is your child going to make sense of their diagnosis, or whatever it is. A lot of this stuff puts the onus on the child. I think our job really is to formulate something that feels okay for them around this stuff. To translate that in a way they can handle and take on board as themselves and absorb into their identity in a helpful way. I think it's a very simplified thing where you say, 'When the classroom's too noisy, you might need a break'. I don't think they need to know, age appropriate as well, but I don't think they need to be loaded down with all this stuff. As a parent, it's a weight, like a lot of diagnoses. And then there's a ton of information around the diagnoses to take in.

This is slightly off-piste, but do you think it would be incredibly helpful – if you could smash the system up and start again – one thing would be to add in that people could access an EP more, because I think this is the other thing, we only get to see EPs usually when we're starting this process.

I think we assume the professional is going to have the

answer and actually we need to tap into our own 'toolbox' if you like. To work out what it is and articulate that.

Abi: I think it can be quite hard to work out what it is you're doing, can't it?

Eliza: It's about finding a way that you can feel a bit more empowered, I suppose, isn't it, as a parent with this stuff? We put a lot on that professional to solve it, but we do know our child best. If we can find a way to tap into what those things are then there's more chance of whatever the school put in place working. The more you can share about what works, then the more they're going to be able to respond.

I think this is a problem as well, because the parent has to share more than they want to share in this situation. Because they're trying to convince the school, they are then going to overexpose themselves by sharing in this situation.

Abi: It's very overexposing for parents isn't it. Having to show how difficult it is, and then the fear?

Eliza: You're always scared of being judged for how you're responding, and it being about you.

CHAPTER 4

PREPARING TO REQUEST AN ASSESSMENT

Toby wasn't sure whether to apply for an EHCP for his child, Jay. Toby had adopted Jay and from everything he knew about his experiences before living with him, he was expecting him to need additional support throughout school. Other parents he knew in similar circumstances were going through the process already and Toby wanted to make sure he was doing everything he could for him. The GP was also suggesting that Jay would have long-term needs and an EHCP would be necessary. But at school, they felt that he was doing okay academically and had enough support. They warned Toby that he probably would get turned down by the local authority and advised him to wait and see how Jay developed. Toby didn't know what to do and whose advice to follow.

Deciding whether you need to apply for an EHCP is hard. Deciding when the right time is to apply can also be hard. Add to that the conflicting messages around what is necessary in order to apply, and it's easy to see why you might be feeling confused, frustrated, and a bit lost.

Local authority policies and procedures make particular requirements of schools when they make an application for an assessment, for valid, understandable reasons. Local authorities turn down applications if they don't meet their criteria and follow their policies. However, according to the SEN Code of Practice (DfE & DoH, 2015), the legal bar for conducting an assessment is as follows:

> **The law says...**
> If both of these are true, then legally the LA has to assess them:
>
> - if your child **may** have SEN
> - if they **may** need additional provision.

This means that if your child might have special educational needs, the local authority has a duty to assess them, regardless of their own policies and procedures. Whilst your child might not meet the criteria for assessment according to the local authority, you probably do meet the legal criteria for assessment. In practice, this might mean the school SENCO says your child doesn't have a high enough level of need, and doesn't qualify for an EHCP, but your child would qualify for an assessment according to the law.

Rita talks here about her experience deciding to apply for an EHCP, and the different messages she received.

> My child has development delays. When she was at nursery, she was under the Child Development Centre and through them we had portage initially and then we had physio, OT, and speech and language, which were great. She was offered a two-year placement at nursery and I immediately said yes, great, can we have an EHCP? They said no one who goes to mainstream nursery gets an EHCP. Someone else said that's not the law, that's policy. I've heard that sentence, that phrase, hundreds of times since. That's not law, that's policy. We did a parental request for a needs assessment because the nursery didn't want to do it. We knew someone

> who was able to help us with the law for free. We went to tribunal and the local authority caved at the point at which they have to respond to your appeal. After that, it was fine, she was in mainstream school, and we did the annual review every year.

Rita knew that EHCPs were available to children from birth, but her local authority had a policy that children under five didn't need one. She decided she wanted to have an EHCP in place before her child started school, so they had all the support available to them straightaway. If your child has good support in place when they are younger, you might be happy to wait for them to develop more, and see how their skills develop. You might want to wait because their needs may change and their difficulties might become clearer.

School and nursery staff work within the structures of the local authority. When they advise you about what you and the school need to apply, they will be working within the policy.

Example of local authority requirements for an EHCNA assessment:

- Child needs to have evidence of intervention over three terms.
- Child needs to have evidence of how additional funding is being spent.
- Child needs to be behind academically by more than two years.

Is that law or policy?

The local authority will have policies in place to help them decide which children are most in need, and where to direct their resources. Resources and funding are always in demand. These policies help them prioritise and help ensure the school has put support in place for children, and used the funding they have available, before asking for extra help. Policies and procedures are liable to change and are different in different local authorities. The law is national and remains consistent for longer periods.

It can be hard to discern what is policy or procedure and what is the law when it is all new to you.

Here are some examples of what you might hear. These are examples of policy or procedure, not law:

- Children under five do not get EHCPs.
- Children need to be two years behind academically to get a plan.
- The school needs to show evidence they are spending £6,000 on SEN support for the child.
- You need evidence that external professionals have been involved.
- SEN support has to be in place for at least three terms before you can apply.
- EHCPs are only for children who are behind academically.

The statements above are all policy but they are not written in law. This means that if you apply for a needs assessment and the local authority said it won't assess your child, you can take your case to a tribunal, which would make their decision based on the law. The tribunal would probably decide to assess your child.

> We were refused an assessment and the reason they gave was that he wants to go to university, so an EHCP is not required. I had a really good diagnostic report that identified a lot of stuff. We went to mediation and overturned that decision. I made no bones about how unlawful this was. He wants to go to uni isn't a valid reason not to assess.

When is the right time to apply?

When to apply is often something that worries people. It can help to know that you don't just have one opportunity, you can reapply. You might be worried whether your child will be able to cope with the new context, such as in Year 5/6 in preparation for secondary school. There are certain points in the system when expectations increase and children are expected to be more independent, such as the beginning of Year 1, the transition to secondary school and starting Year 9. If you apply in advance, you have the reassurance of knowing all the information about your child is on record, and will be transferred properly, and additional thought and professional expertise will be given to how to meet their needs and which placement is suitable for them. If you decide to wait, you might avoid the hassle of the application, and you might find they flourish in the new environment and adapt in ways you didn't foresee. You may find the resources of the new school are able to meet their needs better.

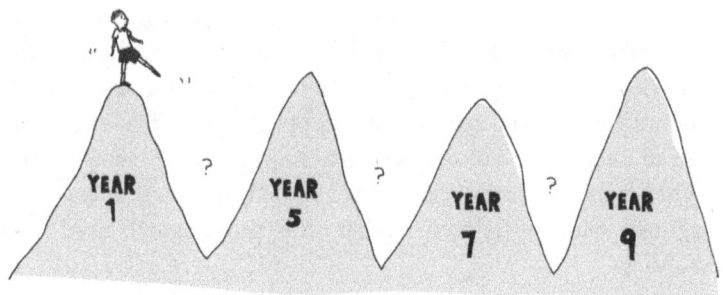

> I wasn't very aware of EHCPs and what they actually entailed and what they meant. I had to self-educate massively because no one ever said to me go and apply, if you did that would help, we'd get funding, if we get funding we can support her more. The local authority says you don't need an EHCP because the school should do this, but the school are not doing it. You have to take the local authority to court because there's no other way of getting the school to do it.
>
> School wouldn't support getting an EHCP. They kept saying, no, you won't get it. Even support services wouldn't support because she's functioning, she's academically bright. I said she's just coping, if she had support, she would thrive. I put in the request for assessment and it went backwards and forwards for months, they refused to assess. I kept quoting the same, the legal test is 'may or may not have SEND needs'. I had to put it in for tribunal. Once it got to the LA legal team, they said we'll assess.

Gathering evidence of your child's needs

When your child has a high level of support in school, but perhaps isn't progressing, or needs more resources, then school will start to document meetings and gather evidence of their needs, in case the decision is made to apply for a needs assessment. If you know you want an assessment, you should check they are doing this.

Schools can choose how they document children's special needs, so there is no prescribed approach. Sometimes this gathering evidence process is quick and focused, but sometimes it is hard to discern what your child needs, there are challenges in understanding what might help, and school and parents disagree. It is often quite hard to decide when and whether to request an assessment. You might have discussions with school staff about whether getting a diagnosis would be helpful, or what other professionals need to be involved.

Evidence school could provide includes:

- Provision map which explains what your child receives at school that is additional and different, with detailed costs
- A 'passport' or 'one page profile' which summarises their needs and strategies which help
- Notes from meetings with you/professionals
- Details of any support tried (e.g. an extra literacy group and how they have helped or not
- Attainment data (test results, levels of achievement, e.g. EYFS, Key Stage 1 or 2 tests, exams)
- Internal assessments and observations, e.g. dyslexia screening, sensory checklist
- External assessments/advice from other professionals

Seeking further advice and support

The following tables offer ways of thinking about what your child is finding hard at school. There are six, covering executive functioning, emotional regulation, physical skills and differences, cognitive development and learning, language, communication and social development, and sensory differences. I explain what these terms mean at the beginning of each table.

The first column is what you might see, or school might be concerned about. You might want to highlight or tick the ones which you feel are relevant for your child. The second column explains the broader area and skills where they are struggling. The third column gives you some ideas of the factors that can contribute to or underlie difficulties in this area. The final column highlights some of the ways in which schools can make this difficulty hard for a child or young person to manage.

Executive functioning

You can think of executive functioning as like the control centre in our brain. These skills are important to help us to manage and coordinate ourselves. Children and young people develop these skills at different rates and if they have other differences, it can take longer or be harder for them.

My child...	What are we talking about?	Factors which might affect or underlie this difficulty/difference	Why might this be hard at school?
Doesn't start work Isn't doing homework Is very forgetful Is very impulsive Is easily distracted and off task Doesn't want to stop doing things/change activity Doesn't like changes to routine or plans Takes more physical risks than others Disruptive/challenging behaviour	Difficulty in organising, planning, and sequencing their work/activities Difficulty in managing their time Difficulty in maintaining concentration Difficulties in self-control and self-monitoring Difficulty in thinking flexibly	Sleep deprivation Ongoing high stress levels Anxiety Changes at home Sensory differences Immature for their age Within normal range of development Genetic inheritance Traumatic brain injury	Length of time sitting still Fewer breaks Busy or noisy classroom environment Frequent transitions Frequent changes in task Not able to make their own choices Not ready to function independently and manage themselves Not ready to work independently and manage homework etc.

Emotional regulation

This is the ability to manage our emotions and soothe ourselves. Children and young people are all learning how to do this. Other difficulties, with peers, school work, or the sensory environment of school might mean it is much harder for some children than others.

PREPARING TO REQUEST AN ASSESSMENT

My child...	What are we talking about?	Factors which might affect or underlie this difficulty/difference	Why might this be hard at school?
High levels of anxiety Meltdowns at home Gets very upset and takes a long time to calm down Not wanting to go to school Is disruptive Fights with peers Angry outbursts Doesn't want to leave me (separation anxiety) Withdrawing from activities and people Has stopped communicating with me Says they feel unhappy/sad all the time Complains of physical symptoms such as lethargy and fatigue, feeling sick, stomach aches, or panic attacks Is staying in their bedroom	Difficulty keeping yourself on an even keel Difficulty calming yourself down Difficulty identifying what you are feeling Difficulty talking about feelings	School-related anxiety Ongoing high stress levels Language difficulties Difficulties with school work Difficulties with peers Changes at home Sensory differences Immature for their age Normal developmental stage Biological pre-disposition Traumatic experiences Changes at school Changes at home Moving house Transitions at school New teachers Difficulties in friendships Problems with school work Unidentified learning problems Unidentified language difficulties Testing and exam pressures	Lack of supportive adult at the right time Lots of peer interaction all day Lots of transitions Lots of adult direction Harder to access calming activities Adults might not know how to respond/support Not enough quiet time during the day

Physical skills and differences

Children develop physical skills at different times, and according to the experiences they've had. Some children have physical disabilities from birth. Impairments with vision or hearing are not always obvious so it is worth having this checked if you are concerned.

My child...	What are we talking about?	Factors which might affect or underlie this difficulty/ difference	Why might this be hard at school?
Is very active Finds it hard to stay still Finds writing painful Has illegible writing Can't do physical activities others can, e.g. ride a bike yet Can't use scissors or cutlery, tie their shoelaces Finds sitting upright painful	Gross motor skills Fine motor skills Visual impairments Hearing impairments Physical disabilities requiring equipment or an accessible environment	Normal range of developmental difference Not yet had enough opportunity to develop the muscles or practice the activity (they may need more than others) Difference from birth Accident or injury Childhood condition, e.g. glue ear Unidentified vision or hearing differences Finds it hard to control how much pressure they use, e.g. makes holes in paper with pencil	Behaviours may be misconstrued as naughty or lazy Lots of writing Lots of sitting Comparison with peers who are further ahead can be hard School building might not be fully accessible Staff may not fully understand the impact of an impairment The impact of the impairment can be invisible to their peers and new staff May not be able to take part in all activities – can be socially isolating

Cognitive development and learning

Children develop at different rates and learning is not linear over time. Sometimes schools can expect everyone to move steadily at the same pace, and it can be problematic if this is not the case. Executive functioning skills and their ability to organise themselves can particularly impact on how a child learns in the classroom environment.

PREPARING TO REQUEST AN ASSESSMENT

My child...	What are we talking about?	Factors which might affect or underlie this difficulty/difference	Why might this be hard at school?
Is behind in their reading Isn't doing enough writing Is struggling with maths Isn't making expected progress Is not enjoying school Is scared of getting it wrong Is misbehaving at a low level all the time Isn't engaged in learning Isn't doing their homework	Reading skills Writing skills Maths skills Other curricular subjects Reasoning ability Non-verbal reasoning ability	Children develop at different rates and learning is not linear over time Dislike of reading because of pressure to read Dislike of writing because lots of writing is required Speaking additional languages (may delay English language skills initially) Fine motor difficulties Specific learning difficulties Language difficulties Writing skills always lag behind reading skills	Curriculum moving too quickly Curriculum mismatched to their level Teaching methods and resources which are not engaging them Emphasis on getting things 'right' Competition within the class Frequent testing Lack of alternatives to writing, e.g. audio recording, scribe, practical activities Activities which lack purpose and interest Didactic approaches to teaching Lack of personal relationship with teacher

Language, communication, and social development

This table encompasses understanding (reciprocal) language, speaking (expressive) language, and social communication and interaction. The important thing to realise about language difficulties (or differences) is that they impact on everything else at school. When a child is struggling to understand language, or interact with their peers, this will impact them in many different ways in the classroom, affecting their relationships and their learning. This is a very broad area, so it is not comprehensive.

My child...	What are we talking about?	Factors which might affect or underlie this difficulty/ difference	Why might this be hard at school?
Finds it hard to have a back-and-forth conversation Finds it hard to understand jokes, sarcasm or language idioms Has a limited vocabulary for their age Appears to understand but then can't complete a task Doesn't talk at school Doesn't make eye contact Doesn't follow instructions unless they are explained one-to-one Sees things as black and white and takes things literally Is always on their own at break time Gets into fights with others Has intense interest in one thing Stammers or avoids saying some words Has difficulty with social interactions with people they don't know Can't take turns Finds it hard to make friends	Differences in communication Differences in understanding and processing language Differences in social interaction	Non-verbal communication differences Pronunciation and articulation difficulties Differences in social communication Within normal range of development On a different developmental trajectory to their school peers Differences in processing language (takes them longer) Anxiety Language delay for another reason, e.g. early experiences	Social interaction and complex language all day Difficulties with speech and language affect a child's writing and their wider participation at school Affects peer interactions and makes forming friendships harder Lots of quick, verbal instructions given to the whole class Lots of language to process all day Not enough time to process instructions Noisy and busy environment Lots of transitions Not able to make their own choices Requirements for eye contact Having different interests from peers makes friendships harder Working in small groups or pairs without support

Sensory differences

Children can be more or less sensitive than is typical to everyday stimuli. Children who are very sensitive might find it intolerable to be near a smell for example. They might find the label on clothing, or the position of their socks intolerable. If they are very sensitive to common everyday stimuli, they might be constantly stressed by things at school, which can mean they are more likely to be distressed and struggle emotionally.

My child...	What are we talking about?	Factors which might affect or underlie this difficulty/ difference	Why might this be hard at school?
Hates certain smells

Only eats a very small range of foods

Hates loud noises

Will only wear certain fabrics/ clothes

Really likes spinning, swinging, jumping, pushing against things and does this more than other children

Finds it hard to calm down and gets very upset

Can hit others when they get upset

Is having meltdowns at the end of the day | Different sensitivities to everyday stimuli, e.g. smell, sound, touch, taste

Differing awareness of their body in space, and their own strength and control of this | Differences in sensory processing

Normal developmental stage

Within normal spectrum of physical activity

Exacerbated by the environment | Leaving foods might not be okay

Desired food might not be available

Child may not eat or drink all day

Uniform may cause discomfort

Strong smells around toilets, dining hall

Child may avoid going to the toilet

Noises like school bell

Overstimulating environment

Harder to access calming activities |

Assessments and diagnoses

Your child might have been seen by other professionals before you have reached this point of considering applying for an EHCNA (needs assessment), but they might not. If you want advice from an expert in a particular area, then the first step is to speak with your GP, health visitor, or your child's school or nursery. They will give you a sense of your child's difficulties in relation to their age, and put this in the context of their life experiences so far.

You often need a referral to seek help from other professionals in the education or health system. This usually comes from your GP, another health professional, or your child's nursery or school. If you want the GP to make the referral, you will need to explain your concerns about your child's development and ask for a referral for an assessment. If nursery/school think an assessment might be helpful, they can write a letter to your GP, or sometimes they can make the referral themselves. The SENDCO and GP will listen to your concerns, and also make their own observations and gather information, to help consider whether how your child is behaving and what they are struggling with falls within what is considered 'typical' development for that age. If you are not sure what to say to the GP or school, the table above offers some ideas.

If you are considering seeing a professional privately, then you don't need a referral, though it still can be helpful to have another perspective from the GP or school. An educational psychologist will think about your child as a whole, and in the context of their environment, if school are involved. If your child has needs in several areas, an educational psychologist is probably a good place to start, though they are more expensive and harder to find. Their assessment is holistic, so they will look at everything your child is struggling with, and draw out how that impacts them in the classroom and make recommendations to help.

Services like speech and language therapy or occupational therapy can both assess children and offer therapeutic intervention. This means they see your child over time and help them develop their skills in a particular area. Your school might also have access to support from specialist schools, or a social communication difficulties service, such as an autism specialist. There are lots of different ways of thinking about what children struggle with, and professionals have expertise in different areas.

This diagram illustrates the general process for seeking further assessment through the education or health system.

General process for seeking an assessment in health or education

What happens at an assessment?

Assessments are a way of finding out more about what is going on for your child. They can be helpful, bring clarity to a child's difficulties, and provide recommendations for school and home. They are, at least in part, a comparison with other children of the same age, highlighting ways your child is different and what they're struggling with.

Assessments often take place away from school – in a clinic, so they can be divorced from normality and they are in a false setting, where your child may or may not feel at ease. Assessments are often one-off events, which culminate in a long report. They may include strengths and difficulties, but their purpose is to highlight what the problems are.

At an assessment they will ask you about your child's development, and when they achieved their milestones such as starting to talk. They will watch how your child plays and interacts. They might do some tests, games, or fun activities with your child. It is best if you don't have other children with you, and if there is someone else who can look after your child elsewhere whilst you talk.

They might ask you questions about:

- what you're concerned about
- what your child's development has been like since they were a baby
- how your child behaves with people they know well/don't know well
- how they like to play, what they like doing
- any physical or health issues, or issues with toileting, eating, or sleeping
- how they communicate
- how nursery/school is going.

Would it help if my child had a diagnosis?

You might be wondering whether having a diagnosis would help your child to get support. Some assessments, such as for ADHD or autism, are called 'diagnostic assessments', and you might be placed on a 'diagnostic pathway'. Other assessments don't necessarily result in a diagnosis, but provide more information about what a child is struggling with, and offer recommendations to help.

Sometimes parents think they have to get a diagnosis to apply, or that if they have a diagnosis it would be easier to get an EHCP. Neither of those is true. You need evidence of what they are struggling with, and one way of getting this can be getting a diagnosis.

PREPARING TO REQUEST AN ASSESSMENT

Having a diagnosis doesn't mean you automatically get a plan, and you don't need to have one in order to get an EHCP. You don't need a diagnosis, you just need evidence of their needs. Evidence could be a letter from the GP, or a school report, or an assessment by the school SENCO.

Issues to consider around diagnostic assessment for your child:

- Your child may or may not get a diagnosis after the assessment, and both experiences can be emotional and take time to process.
- It can take a very long time to get a diagnostic assessment via the NHS.
- Private assessments are very expensive, and are not always accepted by services.
- It can be very validating and reassuring to get a diagnosis as it provides an explanation for your child's difficulties.
- A diagnosis of a neurodevelopmental condition is lifelong. Some adults are not happy that they were diagnosed as children.
- Access to some specialist support services may require a diagnosis before your child will be considered.
- Diagnosis can lead to stigma and labelling which can be limiting and unhelpful.
- Diagnosis can become part of your child's identity and shape their development, in both helpful and unhelpful ways.
- It can provide some clarity and written evidence about your child's struggles.

My child has lots of diagnoses

You might be in the position where your child has multiple diagnoses. Sometimes parents worry about how this will be viewed and it can be hard to make sense of how the diagnoses relate to each other. From my perspective, educational psychologists are used to handling complexity. It is very common to be writing a report for a child with multiple diagnoses. We don't expect to know it all and we are used to learning about conditions that we haven't come across before. It is a normal part of our job to go and do some research.

Sometimes a diagnosis doesn't actually tell you very much about what an individual child is struggling with, and how it impacts them in the classroom and their learning. It helps to think about your child as an individual, rather than through the lens of a diagnosis. We need to focus on what their difficulties are and how those difficulties impact them in the classroom. An educational psychology report will focus on what they are struggling with, break that down, and make recommendations to help.

PREPARING TO REQUEST AN ASSESSMENT

There are lots of lists of strategies for different conditions available freely on the internet now. Strategies which school use need to be based on the whole child – and a list of generic ideas can't really do this. There should always be a decision-making process and the strategies should be individualised.

How do I get an assessment for…?

Different professionals are experts in different areas. Some conditions are lifelong diagnoses, such as ADHD and autism. There are sometimes long waiting lists. If you are considering paying for an assessment, be aware that having an assessment doesn't always mean you get a diagnosis, and the professional will give you their professional opinion, they may not say what you want them to say. Some services won't accept assessments which have been paid for privately.

The NICE guidelines, which you can find online, are seen as the 'gold standard' in how assessments should be carried out. For ADHD and autism, this is an assessment with a multi-disciplinary team, which means a team made up of professionals with different skills, such as a paediatrician, a speech and language therapist, an educational psychologist, or a play therapist.

Should we get a private assessment?

Many parents are on a limited budget and reports are very expensive. The majority of parents do not get private reports and there are lots of other ways to get the outcome you want that don't cost money. If it is something you are considering, there are some things to be aware of.

Parents come to me with all sorts of different private reports and they are sometimes really poor quality. Sometimes people say they are experts when they are not, or they use tools they shouldn't. Make sure you check they are registered with the appropriate national body (in the UK it's the HCPC for psychologists and health professionals) and look at their experience. Talk to them before you commission the work. Registration with a professional body means there is someone to complain to if you're not happy with their work, and it also tells you that they work within ethical guidelines. Try and get a recommendation from someone else if you can, school may have contacts, the GP might recommend someone, or other parents may be able to help. It's also worth remembering that you are paying people to give you their professional opinion, and there is no guarantee they will say what you want or expect.

My child didn't get a diagnosis – what does that mean?

It can be hard if you go through the diagnostic process but do not receive a diagnosis. This means there is not enough information to make a diagnosis. Other factors, or the interaction of multiple factors such as developmental delay, language difficulties, or sensory issues, can make it hard to discern what is causing the difficulties. A diagnosis is for life, so professionals might be hesitant to diagnose if they don't think it is clear, or they might disagree with each other. You don't need a diagnosis to get extra help. If your child is having some difficulties, this will be recorded through this process, and you can use that as evidence in the EHCP process.

> Nobody ever sat me down and explained how a diagnosis impacted everything and what I would need to do differently. Nobody ever told me there was this option or that option. It was almost always, you must do X, Y, and Z. You need to talk to other people that have been through it. Local people will tell you how they navigated it, what you're likely to come up against, and where to go for things locally. You need the national helplines and the online training things because you're pushed down the narrative of parenting courses that are out of date.

My child isn't attending school – can I still get an assessment?

Sometimes people think they will be automatically knocked back if they apply and their child isn't in school – and from my experience, that isn't the case. However, the local authority may have limited experience assessing children out of school, so they may not have thought through how to respond and what they can do. Even if you are turned down initially, the local authority has a responsibility to provide an education for your child. If your child can't attend school, you have robust evidence that the school provision didn't work for them.

Your child might be at home and refuse to engage with any professionals. It is certainly harder for professionals to conduct assessments if they can't see the child and can't watch them at school, so it requires creativity and understanding. An educational psychology assessment for an EHCP brings together information from home, school, and direct work with the child. I regularly write reports when I can't speak to or do any activities with the child – I draw on what we know and I use creative approaches, sometimes working through parents, sometimes watching videos or using parental questionnaires – I draw on lots of different forms of evidence.

Other people don't see the problem

You might be finding it hard to get people to understand what your child is struggling with, because it's unseen. Perhaps your child doesn't communicate verbally but you understand their signals of distress better than others. They might think your child is just behaving badly, whilst you know that they are struggling with the sensory environment and don't really understand what's going on. Sometimes if the problems only happen at home, or if they have a hidden health issue such as a brain condition, it can be difficult to work out what's happening. It might also be the case that some aspects of your child's difficulties, such as challenging behaviour, draw a lot of attention and concern, but their underlying difficulties are missed because of this.

I worked with a child called Ioan who was having seizures at school – and when this happened the first few times, they got an ambulance, and there was of course a lot of attention and worry, and the school focused on putting safety plans in place and making sure he would be safe. But because they were so focused on managing the seizures, they didn't really notice some of the other changes which had also happened, like he was struggling to understand some of his work, and he was having new difficulties with processing language. He didn't want anyone to notice, so didn't tell anyone either. I got involved because he was increasingly anxious, and this began to affect him in all areas of his life.

Megan is a ten-year-old I've been working with recently who looks absolutely fine at school. She is very compliant, eager to please and does not want to attract any attention. But at home she's melting down; she's very anxious, saying she wants to die, and is starting to refuse to get in the car to go to school.  She is absolutely exhausted by the effort she's putting in at school, so as not to show anything she doesn't feel she should show.

It's not unusual for children to behave differently at home and school. If a child doesn't feel safe at school, or if they're scared of being ridiculed, or punished, they might start to hide how they feel. They might say they don't need help, even though they do. They might say they're fine, even though they're not. They might pretend to get on with things, even though they don't understand what they're doing. And they might be so good at it that school can't tell. Children can also put on a front when they don't know what to do, or the work is too hard, by playing the clown or just being continually disruptive so they get sent out of the lesson.

I'm not sure school is working

You might be thinking school just doesn't seem like an option for us, or my child is too unwell and anxious to access school. If that's the case, you might need to take a different path altogether. You might need to find out about other schools, or consider education other than at school (EOTAS) or elective home education (EHE). Professionals in the process may not be aware of these options and might not bring them up. Whilst these might not be good options for your family right now, it can help to be aware of them, because at some point those changes might really help.

If you are not ready to make the decisions about those options, there are some things that can be built into EHCPs if you can show they work for your child. These aren't necessarily possible in all contexts, and they may not be commonly in use in your area or your school:

- Building flexibility into the EHCP, e.g. through a reduced timetable, shorter school day
- Flexi-schooling – e.g. two days in, three days at home
- Virtual schooling or home tutoring

COFFEE TIME WITH ABI AND ELIZA

Abi: This is a whole chapter about deciding to apply, because it can take a long time to get off the starting blocks in the EHCP process.

Eliza: Yes, it's confusing! This stuff isn't linear. Often schools seem to expect to see that things are consistently plummeting. And actually, because children do have so much resilience, they will have times where they seemingly bounce back and it is quite contradictory.

Abi: It's normal for it to be up and down.

Eliza: You have to think for yourself, what are the measures that are too much? What will mean that we have to do something really different here? What's the measure that means I have to contact the SENCO?

Abi: And then as well as that, you have the conflicting messages about whether your child needs one or would get one.

Eliza: Yes. Something that will make a huge difference to parents, certainly did for me, was knowing that LAs put policy in that aren't law. It gives you the confidence to push back. Even for myself now, if I was going through it, I'd have to really think, no, the law says this. Everything is saying you don't need one, you won't get anything different. And actually, no one knows what you'll get. Sometimes they push back and say, what would you want to get from it? And you don't know. But I know that this isn't working.

CHAPTER 5

THE EHCP PROCESS

In Chapter 2 we thought about what your child struggles with and what they might need that is additional and different. In Chapter 3 we began to work with school to implement some changes and gather evidence. In this chapter I will walk you through the EHCP process, explain how to make a request for assessment, and what to expect.

What to expect

> Lisa decided she needed to apply for an EHCNA for her son. School said he didn't meet their criteria for an EHCP but she could still apply and see what happened. They helped her go online and showed her how to access the online hub and make the application. The SENCO gave her some examples of what other parents had written when they had applied to help her start. She stuck the timeline up on the fridge so she knew when she should hear from the local authority about whether they were going to assess or not.

THE ESSENTIAL EHCP GUIDE FOR PARENTS AND CARERS

Timeline of the EHCP process

PREPARATION

Gather the information you have, e.g. medical reports, letters, history.
Encourage school to gather data, make observations.
Think about and gather evidence of your child's needs.

Week 0	REQUEST & DECISION MAKING School or parent request an assessment. ↓ LA decision-making panel consider request. ↓ They decide whether or not to assess your child. If they say no, you can offer more evidence or go to mediation or appeal.
Week 6	ASSESSMENT A caseworker requests written advice from: • You • School • Educational psychologist • GP/Paediatrician • Other professionals as approriate/requested
Week 12	DRAFT PLAN The caseworker writes a draft plan, based on the evidence. By Week 16, the LA decides to issue a plan or not. If they decide no, you can appeal. They will write and tell you.
Week 17	CONSULT & FINALISE You review the draft and make suggestions. There is a deadline for this. Caseworker consults with possible school placements. Schools have 15 days to respond. The final plan is issued.

Managing the process – be a project manager

Elena told me she had decided her role was to project manage the EHCP process. She said at first she'd expected the caseworker to hold her hand and support her through the process, but she realised that wasn't their job. She expected someone to explain the process to her, but they didn't. In the end, she went to parent forums, she talked to other parents

> with children who needed something different, and she did quite a bit of what she called research. She found out what the options were, and decided what she thought would work best. Once she'd realised she needed to project manage, she put the legal timelines in her diary. She kept records – so she had a big file of reports and notes from meetings. She called the SEN caseworker weekly to politely check in.

How do I apply?

If you want to apply yourself, there is a template you can download. You don't have to send anything additional with this. Some local authorities will direct you to an online hub to do the process electronically, but you are always within your rights to just send a letter or email to start the process. The first thing the LA will do when they get your request is contact the school to ask for more information, ask how your child is doing academically and what school have in place to support them. If school make the request they will fill in all the forms and send this information directly.

It is usually considered better if an application comes from school, as this means they have already thought about your child. They will also handle all the paperwork, and are familiar with the language and how to present all the information, which takes the pressure off you. However, as I've explained, school do have to satisfy a higher level of proof than a parent. I've worked with a parent whose SENCO told her to make the application, because she knew that the application was more likely to be accepted that way.

Requesting an assessment

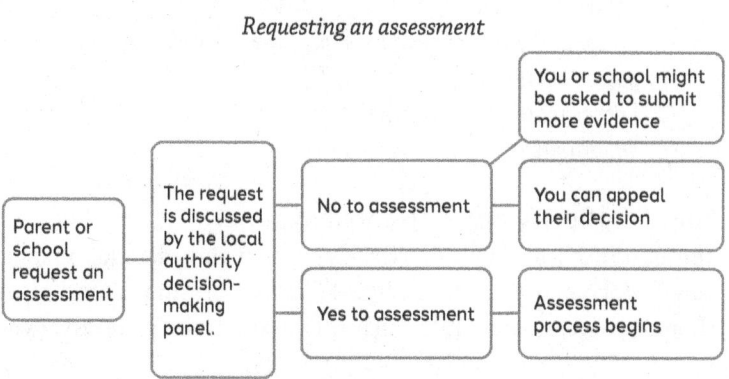

Local authorities have their own policies which detail specific things they ask a school to do, and show evidence of, before they make a request for an assessment. Schools have SEN funds which they use for children with SEN to put support in place before doing an application. Local authority policies are a way of ensuring this money is being well spent, before they allocate more for an individual child. Typically local authorities want to see evidence of your child's needs and evidence that the school understands their needs. They want to know school have tried things, and that they had done everything they can, before asking for help. Sometimes local authority policies become very constrictive and can exclude lots of children from having an assessment, for example saying you can only apply for an EHCP if your child is two years behind academically. In these circumstances, parents need to apply themselves, as this requirement is much more stringent than the law (see Chapter 2).

Reasons you might give:

- Not making progress despite interventions in place
- Needs more specialist teaching
- Needs individual support beyond what school offers
- Needs therapies from speech and language
- Needs specialist equipment (e.g. sensory room)

Evidence you might have:

- Reports and assessments from school over time
- Notes from meetings
- School information about what they are providing for your child
- Reports from professionals, e.g. speech and language, occupational therapy
- Letter from GP or paediatrician
- Diagnosis letter/private reports

Local authority decision-making panel

The local authority will have a weekly or fortnightly decision-making panel which meets to decide how EHCNA assessments and plans should progress. Your child will be discussed at the panel after you have requested an assessment. The local authority has six weeks after they have received the request to make a decision about whether to conduct an assessment. All the paperwork you and school send in will be available to the panel. If you have submitted the request, the LA will request the information they need from school.

Key points in the EHCP process (from Disabled Children's Partnership, Jemal and Kenley, 2023)

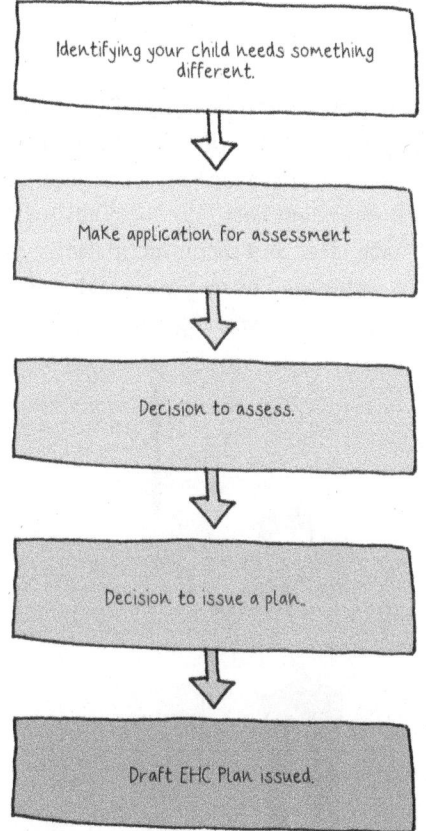

The panel is made up of professionals who work for the local authority, and the mix of professionals will vary in different authorities. It would certainly include members of the special educational needs team; they act as the meeting chair and your caseworker would normally be there to summarise your child's case. There is usually a representative from the educational psychology service, and representatives from a local special school and local mainstream school. There could also be a representative from the specialist teaching service, health care, social care, and early years.

Your child's case will be brought to the decision-making panel at various points during the assessment and plan-writing process. The panel is usually involved in decisions such as whether to grant an assessment, whether to issue a plan and the most appropriate setting.

What school/provision is right for your child?

What are you hoping for? What do you think your child needs? You care the most about this decision and what happens next for your child, and you know them best. The local authority and the professionals will have ideas and recommendations, but many of the decisions can be influenced by you and what you think will work. Part of the EHCP process is working out what the next step is.

At some point in the process, you will be asked which school you would like your child to go to. If no one asks you, then I would bring it up yourself. It's good to think about the options early on and develop a realistic vision. It's rare for someone in the local authority to sit you down and talk you through all the options – it's best to do some research yourself, talk to other parents, ask questions, and visit some local options. It is a good idea to ask your caseworker which schools they are considering for your child.

A good place to start for your local options is SENDIAS – they're funded by the local authority but they are independent, and are specifically to support parents. They are often staffed by parents with children with special educational needs, who have been through the EHCP process. The schools available vary according to where you live. If an ideal provision appears full, don't be put off, sometimes there are still spaces.

Go and visit a potential school and imagine your child there. You might want to talk to the head or SENCO about your child, and see if you are able to be honest, and how they respond. If you can't tell them honestly what your child is like, then it's unlikely to be successful. Talk to the teachers you meet about the other options. Ask the professionals you meet for ideas.

> Things to think about on school visits:
>
> - How many staff in the classroom?
> - How many children in the class?
> - How do you feel in the school/classroom?
> - Can you imagine your child there?
> - How noisy is it?
> - Where else in school would your child go?
> - Do they have quieter areas?
> - Do they have a fun playground, any other outdoor areas, e.g. Forest School, nature area?
> - How do they manage children's behaviour?
> - What is the school ethos/motto – do you like it?

If you are trying to decide between different options, it can feel overwhelming and like a big responsibility that you really want to get right for your child. A good place to start is a list of the pros and cons.

Parents often face a decision between a local mainstream school or a specialist setting which is further away. If you would like your child to stay in a mainstream school, but with a package of support, then look around at the different options. Think about what can be added to their mainstream experience to tailor it to their interests and needs. If your child is already doing something which works really well out of school, ask if it could happen in school time, as part of their package. It's quite common for young children to start school at their local mainstream primary, before deciding whether to move to a specialist setting or not.

Tom and Gail's daughter Nell has a global developmental delay and communication difficulties. She is four and is due to start primary school in September. They are trying to decide what the best school option is for her, and their family.

Tom and Gail's pros and cons list:

	Specialist setting	**Mainstream local primary**
Pros	Access to speech and language therapy on-site Smaller class sizes Very varied peer group Bespoke curriculum Staff who are used to working with children with her difficulties	Same school as her sister Local community and possible local friendships All walk there altogether Short journey She would be with some of the same children she knows from nursery
Cons	An hour away Would need a taxi journey Peers have a really wide range of needs Wouldn't meet other local children Wouldn't be at the same school as her older sibling	Might not be able to stay here beyond Year 2/3 as curriculum will be too different May not have additional staff to support Teacher isn't used to working with children with communication difficulties Staff are not familiar with the picture communication system Nell uses

Making decisions about which is the best option is always hard and there are always compromises. Doing some research and visiting some schools will help you to make the best decision you can. There are lots of factors to weigh up, and often the journey to and from school and how you will manage that, taking into account where other members of the family need to be for work or school, is a significant factor.

Tom and Gail decided to send Nell to the specialist setting, because they wanted staff who were already experienced in using the communication system Nell uses, and they felt it would be better for her to make the transition now, when other children were also starting at the school, rather than move again in a few years. They found she could share a taxi with another child who was going from the local area.

Types of school
According to the SEN Code of Practice (DfE & DoH, 2015), you have the right to request a particular school, college or other institution of the following type to be named in their EHC plan:

- Maintained nursery school
- Maintained school and any form of academy or free school (mainstream or special)
- Non-maintained special school
- Further education or sixth form college
- Independent school or independent specialist colleges which have been approved by the Secretary of State (this list is called Section 41 and you can find it online)

This is not a comprehensive list of types of provision available. Each area will have different options.

Mainstream schools
Mainstream schools are those which cater to everybody. They vary a lot in what they offer and how they think, so it is worth researching several. These schools might have an SEN hub where young people can go for some time out, or during unstructured times. Primary

schools might have a nurture group that is well established. They might have specially trained staff, or learning mentors.

Once your child has an EHCP, mainstream schools will look at the difficulties listed there to decide if they can meet your child's needs. They are allowed to say they cannot meet your child's needs, if for example they don't think they can educate your child alongside their peers, or it would require too many resources.

Specialist units attached to mainstream schools

There are also mainstream schools with specialist units, often for children with autism, or social communication difficulties. Children and young people can be based in the unit, with a higher staff ratio who have specialist training, and go into mainstream lessons according to what works for them. An advantage of this arrangement is being part of a bigger peer group, and having access to the resources and subject expertise of a larger school. Packages can also be more flexible and adapt as they grow and develop.

Specialist schools

Specialist schools (or special schools) cater to children with particular difficulties, such as autism or learning difficulties. They tend to cater for children with more complex difficulties, who cannot be effectively supported in mainstream schools. These schools may have a range of professionals working on-site, such as speech and language therapists, occupational therapists, and physiotherapists. They have higher staff and assistant ratios, with smaller class groups. The children and young people often have highly bespoke timetables and curriculums.

Independent specialist school

Sometimes there is no maintained specialist school option in your area, but there are appropriate independent options. The government have made a list of approved schools, which you are allowed to request in an EHCP plan. You can find the list online. They are approved under Section 41 of the Children and Families Act (2014), so the list is sometimes called the 'Section 41 list'.

Alternative provision

This is a term for a range of provisions, which are intended to be temporary but often end up being long-term placements. These settings include pupil referral units and medical tuition (alternative tuition for medical reasons).

EOTAS (education other than at school)

EOTAS has grown in its use in the past few years, as more children have struggled to attend school. With an EOTAS package the local authority provides a bespoke package for your child or young person. Local authorities may agree this approach as a short-term measure, with the intention that your child will then go back into an educational setting.

Packages can include a wide range of options, including things which are of particular interest to your child – so they might include some tutoring, some OT, some speech and language, specialist equipment, other therapies. You would need to show that school has failed for your child, and there is no local school that can meet their needs. You will have to provide evidence of your child's needs which mean that none of the available schools are suitable. You may need to appeal and go to tribunal to get it (see Chapter 7) so it can be a long journey. It's important to factor all of those things into your decision making, as the long-term stress of fighting the local authority can have an impact on your family. Managing an EOTAS package in itself can be very stressful, especially if your child has significant needs and is struggling.

EHE (elective home education)

Home education usually means you take on all financial responsibility for your child's education, both cost and content. You would have contact with the home education team, and complete annual reports for them. You can de-register your child from school, though in some circumstances children remain on roll, and there is a school named on the EHCP. You don't need an EHCP to home educate your child, though you might have one. If your child has an EHCP and is in a special school, and you want to take them out, you need local authority permission to do this. There is a lack of official guidance in this area, and individual situations are often complex and unique.

How do I get my views heard and influence the process?

Your child's needs are written based on evidence – this comes from the professionals' assessments, school's information, and from what you say in your written contribution, which is called Section A. If you are near the end of the process and feel your views aren't being heard, or something has changed, you can often add information to Section A.

The meetings with the professionals are good opportunities for you to make your voice heard – so have a think in advance about what you think is important for your child. Go without your child if you can, so you can have a proper discussion, without your child listening or needing your attention. Written evidence from professionals carries a lot of weight in the EHCP process. Have a think about any goals they have for themselves, or what you consider important. It really helps for you to go to those meetings with ideas and points you have thought about, because then your views will be put into those reports, making them stronger and more relevant.

It is much easier to address concerns with professionals earlier in the process. It's helpful if you can read their reports before they are submitted to the local authority, or if not, at least before the EHCP is finalised. If they won't have time to send you a draft, you could ask that they call you to let you know what they think, particularly if it has been hard to have a conversation because your child was present. That way, if there is something specific you think is needed, you will have space to talk about it.

It is helpful to understand the role of the professional you are meeting with so you have some understanding of what they specialise in and the sorts of support they might recommend. There are some case studies at the end of this chapter.

Writing your contribution

Section A is for your views and your child's views. You submit it right at the beginning of the process, and you can usually add things here later on as well, if you realise there is something you've forgotten, or something changes. This section is where you have the most control and you can tell your story. You can explain things, for example if your child has a diagnosis they might not be familiar with, and you can explain how their needs impact on your lives. Local authorities often have a form with questions which you can use if you like, or you can write it however you wish.

> Tips for writing your contribution:
>
> - Don't worry about using specialist language, or getting it 'right'
> - Tell them honestly how it is for you and your family
> - It is fine to use bullet points
> - Headings can help with organising information
> - You can write however you choose – answer the LA questions or write as you prefer
> - Try and avoid repetition
> - Focus on your child and what is going on for them
> - It is much easier to read if you type it

Ideas about what to write:

- Key points about your child's development, e.g. any problems in pregnancy, birth, early learning and developmental milestones
- Any life events which were significant, e.g. moving schools, moving house, bereavements, new siblings, adoption, foster care
- What your child is good at, and what they struggle with
- What your child enjoys, and anything they really don't like
- What support you think they need
- You could talk about a typical day for them
- Their friendships and relationships with teachers
- Their health, their independence and self-help skills
- How they communicate

Helen was really worried about writing the parent contribution for the EHCP. She didn't want to let her son down by not doing it well enough, but she didn't know what to write and she had never been any good at writing at school. Eventually she asked the SENCO at school for help and they sat down together to do it. They kept it simple, and wrote it in three sections: what he is good at, what he struggles with and what support and placement Helen would like for him.

> Max loves gardening and sports. He is really good at football. He has loved the woodwork he has done at school. He enjoys playing with his brothers and cousins.
>
> Max struggles to sit still for long periods at home and school. He has been excluded from his previous school. He gets very angry very quickly when things seem unfair to him, and it is very hard to reason with him. Max has always found it harder than other children to manage his feelings.
>
> The joint placement which Max has at the special school and mainstream school is working really well and I would like this

to continue. He gets different things from each school. He needs the work to be adapted for him so he can do the tasks. He needs people working with him to use humour and to get to know him so he trusts them.

Your child's views

In most circumstances, school staff will support your child to express their views about what they would like. This doesn't have to happen on one occasion, and can take place over time. If your child is not attending school, you can support them to express their views, and the educational psychologist will also talk to them about it. Some children might not be able to express their views in a meaningful way, so professionals may ask you and others who know them well what they think. You or school staff might gather information over several sessions if that is what suits your child best. This section commonly includes their likes and dislikes, things they are good at, things they want to improve and anything else that is important to them, such as pets or favourite sports. There are structures for this you can find online, commonly called 'All About Me'.

What to expect in the educational psychology assessment

Educational psychologists (EPs) work in schools and other educational settings, with children with a really wide range of difficulties, from birth to 25. EPs have lots of different elements to their work which focuses on supporting children, young people, and education, but this part of their job is enshrined in law. When a child has an EHCNA assessment, they must be assessed by an educational psychologist.

What happens in an EP assessment?

Assessments, especially if they involve a home visit, can feel intimidating. But the educational psychologist is not there to judge your parenting or the cleanliness of your home. There are no right or wrong answers to the questions that they ask, and if you don't know the answer, or find yourself struggling to remember something, there is no need to worry, because it's really common. If you remember something you wish you had said afterwards, you can always contact them.

Assessments vary according to the age of your child and your situation. But you can expect the EP to explain what they are going to do, and they will do some of the following:

- Observation at home or school
- Meet with your child
- Talk to you about your child's history and what they are struggling with
- Assessments/questionnaires with you or/and your child

Educational psychologists have lots of different ways to gather information and learn more about what the problems are. If a child is younger, then I would play with them, join them in an activity they're doing, talk to them about things they are interested in. If they're in school then it will probably include some observation of them in school, and perhaps in a range of contexts – like in a lesson, during unstructured times like break time, or in a small group. I would talk to their teacher and whoever knows them the best.

Depending on the problems, EPs have a range of tools to gather information. They can use cognitive assessments, which look at how your child learns and will rank them against their peers, according to how they perform on tasks. They can also use other tools to learn more about your child's emotional and social development, level of independence, and social and communication skills.

What will they ask me?

- What your child is good at and what they enjoy
- What your child finds hard at home and what helps
- What you want for them in the future
- How they are getting on at school
- Any ideas you have about what helps at school

- Any thoughts you have about what you want next for them in education, e.g. if you want them to move school
- How independent they are, appropriate to their age
- Their friendships and relationships with teachers
- Their attitudes and approach to learning and homework
- They might have some questionnaires for you to complete

What will they write in their report?

An EP report will focus on how your child learns, how their difficulties impact them in the classroom, and what might help. It will include information about how your child learns, their current academic skills and attainments, what helps them learn in the classroom, their peer relationships, their communication skills, independence and self-care skills, and anything else of importance to them.

The educational psychologist's statutory (legal) assessment is really important for the final EHCP. It often forms the basis of the final plan. They won't recommend the school where they think your child should go, but they will make recommendations about how they should be educated. If you have ideas about what might help and a view on where you want your child to be educated, now is your chance to discuss it with them.

If you have concerns about something in the EP report, it's much easier to address concerns directly with them, early in the process. The EP will want to work with you, and they want you to be happy with how things are written in the report. They might not always agree with you, or write what you would like, as their job is to provide their professional opinion, but it is easier and more productive to have a conversation directly with the professional who has written the assessment. If you wait until the EHC draft plan is issued, making changes is more difficult.

Educational psychologists will normally send you a copy of the report as well as submit it to the local authority, but it is worth confirming that they plan to do this, or asking to see a draft. They are operating under strict legal timelines – they will only have six weeks to arrange to meet with you, conduct the assessment with your child, and write the report.

Other professionals

As well as an educational psychologist, it is standard for local authorities to consult the following when they conduct an assessment:

- The head/SENCO of the educational setting where your child attends
- Social care (this isn't an assessment, it is an administrative check)
- Health care professionals who have already had involvement with your child

Professionals are asked about your child's strengths and difficulties, and asked to make recommendations as to what special educational provision they need. Other professionals involved will depend on your child's difficulties, and if there is a particular person outside school who you would like to be consulted, such as a tutor, or group leader, you can request this.

Below are case studies and job descriptions of some of the professionals who might be consulted and might assess your child. If your child has seen the paediatrician in the past, they won't usually arrange a special appointment for the EHCNA assessment. Similarly, if speech and language or occupational therapy have already seen your child recently, they might refer to this, rather than see your child again.

OCCUPATIONAL THERAPIST

Zelda is an occupational therapist, or an OT for short. Occupational therapy helps improve children's skills and develop their independence in daily life.

> Children come and see me for things like struggles with writing, difficulty sitting or holding themselves still, or self-help skills, like using cutlery or the toilet. I help them to develop their skills or adapt how they approach things so they can do what they need to in daily life. Sometimes I advise school about how they can help, or I provide equipment. This can help them be more independent and concentrate more easily in class.
>
> When I meet a child I do assessments to see what they can do, and find out their strengths and weaknesses. I have special equipment they can play on. I often ask questions about children's eating habits, their toileting, bathing, emotional regulation, and likes and dislikes around movement and touch.

PAEDIATRICIAN

> I am a doctor who specialises in children's health and development. Children with a range of developmental difficulties are referred to me via their GP. They might be having difficulties with their learning, development, or behaviour. I can diagnose a wide range of difficulties such as developmental delays, ADHD,

Tourette's, and autism. I will usually do a medical examination, and gather information from parents about the problems. I monitor their growth and development, and can prescribe things to help if needed. I consider areas such as their motor skills, language development, and social skills. Children will often have other medical teams working with them as well, if they have health needs like epilepsy, or diabetes. If they are having sleep problems they might also go to a sleep clinic, or for eating problems they might see a dietician. Sometimes I see children and their parents for individual appointments, but I might also see them as part of a team. Sometimes I will see children regularly throughout their childhood.

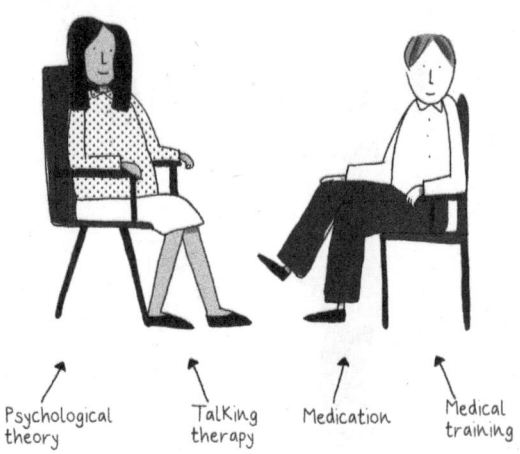

Requesting an EHCNA means you are requesting an assessment with an educational psychologist. Another type of psychologist you might come across is a clinical psychologist. They are trained in psychology but without a medical background. They offer talking therapies such as CBT or EMDR. They might be involved in the autism assessment process, or they might offer parenting help or individual support for you. You might encounter a clinical psychologist if your child is referred to CAMHS (Child and Adolescent Mental Health Services).

SPEECH AND LANGUAGE THERAPIST

Tim is a speech and language therapist.

> I work with children who have speech, language, and communication difficulties. Children are usually referred to me via their GP or sometimes school. Sometimes they will come and see me because they have difficulty making certain sounds. Sometimes they come because they find using and understanding language hard. I might refer them on to see other professionals, or I might work with them in my clinic, or write a programme for school staff to do with them. When I meet a child they often play or read a book whilst I talk to their parent. I can do assessments which look more closely at what parts of language they are struggling with, and how difficult it is for them in comparison to other children.

Physiotherapist

I work in a team for the NHS. I work with children who have physical difficulties, which can arise from a range of different conditions. Sometimes children have a lifelong condition like cerebral palsy, or spina bifida, or they might have a delay in their walking or difficulties with coordination. Our aim is to maximise a child's physical abilities and enable them to participate in activities and be as independent as possible. I often work with a child for a block of sessions and then see them periodically as they grow older. We educate families and education staff about the condition and the support they need and provide a programme of activities to maintain or develop physical skills. We sometimes provide specialist equipment for home and school. We have a child-friendly clinic, and access to a hydrotherapy pool.

Meetings with professionals

Your child's needs are written based on evidence – this comes from the professionals' reports, and from what you say in Section A. Professionals write their opinion from what they see through tests or observations, and they also gather information from you and school. The meetings with the professionals are good opportunities for you to make your voice heard. Think beforehand what you think is important for your child, any goals they have, or what should be prioritised. It really helps for you to go to those meetings with ideas and things you have thought about, because then your views will be put into those reports, and make them stronger and more relevant.

Sometimes parents feel that the professionals are in charge and will make all the suggestions. Professionals have expertise in a particular area, but you are the expert in your child. The professional will bring ideas and professional experience, but the more you can contribute, the better. If you're not sure what the job is of the person you're meeting, it helps to research that beforehand, so you feel more confident.

What the EP writes in their report forms the basis of the final plan. It's much easier to address concerns earlier in the process – so talk to the EP about any concerns before they submit their report. You can ask them to show you the report and send you a draft. All the professionals have to submit their reports within a short, six-week legal deadline, so if you don't receive a draft, that deadline is probably why.

In most circumstances, what the EP writes will become the bulk of the EHCP, so it's really important. They are giving their professional opinion, so you may not agree with everything, and they don't have to make any changes that you request. But I would definitely address any concerns with the EP's report as soon as possible and the EP will want to work with you.

Problem corner
Communication with the local authority

Local authority SEN departments are under a lot of pressure, they have frequent staff changes and lots of staff illness. They may be overwhelmed and their systems may be struggling. If you don't hear from them for long periods, it isn't personal. I worked in local authorities for a long time, so I've seen this from both sides. It is always a good idea to send emails to your case officer and copy in the generic SEN casework email for

your local authority as well, in case your caseworker is off work. You can usually find this easily on the internet if you don't already have it.

The local authority don't recognise my child's diagnosis

Your local authority may have a policy where they don't accept some diagnoses, and they won't write it in your child's EHCP. These diagnoses are those which are not accepted in medical or clinical manuals. A common one which some services won't write in reports is PDA (pathological demand avoidance) which is sometimes given as part of an autism diagnosis. I don't think it is worth fighting about whether they will write a specific term in a report. The important thing is that your child's needs are described clearly, making it clear what your child struggles with (see discussion in Chapter 2). It can help to talk about it with the educational psychologist so they understand what the diagnosis means for your child.

Will the local authority look at private reports?

Sometimes parents worry that private reports won't be accepted by their local authority. In my experience, local authorities do read private reports. They don't have to agree with it all, and different reports will sometimes have differing advice and recommendations. The recommendations which the local authority educational psychologist makes in their report are written with an awareness of the local schools (and other options), and reflect how resources in the local authority are distributed between all children, according to their needs. Private educational psychologists are not constrained in the same way.

Managing the process

It is hard to keep track of the process, particularly if you struggle with organising things or dislike reading large volumes of material. Try and keep track of where you are in the process. Most parents recommend that you keep communication with the local authority written as far as possible, because then you have a record of what has been said, by whom, and when.

- Write things down, or request that others put things in writing.
- Keep records so you don't have to remember things.
- Share the load with someone else if you can.
- Use any tools you might already know well to help manage the process, e.g. Trello, Reminders, Notes.
- SENDIAS (your local independent parent support group) can advise about your own local authority.
- National charities offer free appointments to support parents.
- Facebook groups run by other parents can offer advice gathered by experience.

Finding support

Wren told me about finding a group of mothers through online support groups, who were going through the process at the same time. They were able to ask questions and help each other.

> I found a local mums' support group that was just starting and about eight of us started a little group and that was an absolute lifeline. About three of us were going through tribunal at the same time and it'd be 11 o'clock at night and we'd be all texting each other. What do you do about this, and what should you do when. I don't think I would have coped without that, even with the advocacy services. Sometimes I just need to panic at somebody who gets it, and who knows what I'm talking about, and who knows what Section F means, without having to explain everything. My husband is incredibly supportive but he works full time, I do all of this essentially by myself. He knows enough so he follows along, but he doesn't know it in any detail. Having those friends was what got me through.

COFFEE TIME WITH ABI AND ELIZA

Eliza: Our EHCP, when it was first written in Year 5, was rubbish because I didn't know anything about all this. It was a really wishy-washy EHCP. So in Year 8 we had a reassessment. It was really robust. It meant that all the schools that the LA consulted said no way, we can't accept her. And then we got this independent place.

Abi: And did you already have the independent place in mind, as you were going through it?

Eliza: I didn't know what we were going to do. I was thinking we were going to have to carry on long term with tuition, but I was bored of it and my daughter was bored of it. But the

Abi: LA said, we've got this little place, but it's not in our local authority. They suggested it and it was really good.

Abi: I guess the point is that you don't quite know how the LA is going to respond. And some people will be panicking about not being able to get a particular package or setting, but there are always other options. Their policy might be not what you would initially want, but that doesn't mean that they're not going to look at what your child needs and try and find a good solution.

Eliza: This comes up a lot in consults with families. They will say they're going for a particular thing because they can't find anything else. A lot of families I work with are terrified of trying a setting but you can be surprised at what works. I didn't think we'd make it an hour in a taxi down the road. Your child might be ready to do that. Sometimes people are scared to nudge their children, but if you think it's the right thing, a nudge might be helpful.

Abi: The travel might be hard at the beginning, but it might turn out to be the right thing.

Eliza: If the setting is right, it's not like pushing them back into a mainstream setting where they're going to struggle. Transitions are still going to be tricky, because transitions are hard, but it doesn't mean that where we're going might not be the right thing.

Abi: I guess it's really easy to lose hope as a parent that there is going to be a setting that works.

Eliza: I think also it's important to think about having a child that is growing up. For us, having a child at home who was 11 is very different to them being home at 13. A teenager often wants to be somewhere else.

CHAPTER 6

UNDERSTANDING THE EHCP DOCUMENT

This chapter will help with:

- looking at your child's first draft EHCP
- looking at amendments to a plan, after an annual review or a transition review
- looking at the working document as part of an appeal.

Once all reports have been received, the local authority will prepare a draft EHCP for your child. This will include the sections on your views/your child's views, a summary of their needs and details of the special provisions that are being put in place to help them meet their goals. We will discuss each of these sections in more detail in the next chapter.

Reading the draft plan

Reading an EHC plan can be tough. They can use very stark and direct language and can sound very negative about your child. Reports may explicitly compare your child with how peers of their own age are doing – in whatever way that's possible. When I worked for the local authority, I had to make direct comparisons of where a child was academically in comparison with their peers – recording all their academic levels, their age, and their rate of progress, and assessing whether it was extremely slow, or very slow, or just slow. It was the opposite of a positive, strengths-based approach, but the local authority needed that information in order to decide how high the level of need was, and compare this with the other children who were also requesting extra help.

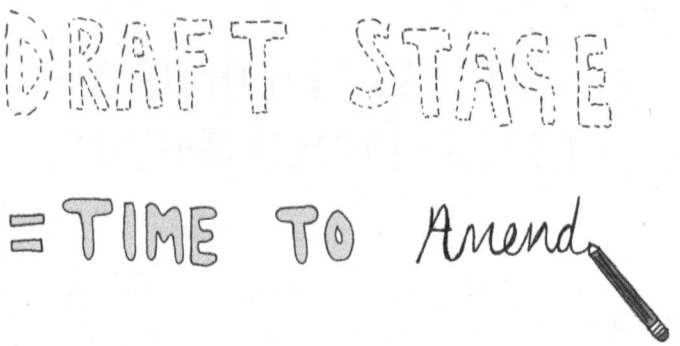

The EHCP document

There are 12 sections in an EHCP and they are all legally required. Local authorities may organise the information differently, and you can look at your own local template online so you know what to expect, but the content is the same.

- Section A: The views of you and your child/young person
- Section B: Your child's special educational needs
- Section C: Your child's health needs, related to their SEN or disability
- Section D: Social care needs related to their SEN or disability
- Section E: Outcomes
- Section F: Special educational provision
- Section G: Health provision
- Section H1 and H2: Social care provision
- Section I: Name and type of the school or institution
- Section J: Personal budget
- Section K: List of all the reports and advice gathered during the assessment

Section A – Your contribution

Section A includes your contribution, and your child's views. It might include information about your child's history, a summary of how to communicate with them, their likes and dislikes, and any plans or goals they have for the future, appropriate to their age. If you haven't done this yet, don't worry as you can still write it now. There is advice about how to approach writing it in Chapter 4, and someone at school could help you if you want. Section A isn't legally binding but it informs the rest of the plan.

If you have made several written submissions for Section A, then check the correct information is included. These sections are normally included exactly as they were written. If something has changed – perhaps you've learned new information, or now you see things differently – you can still add this to Section A at this stage.

Section B – Special educational needs

Section B is a description of your child's special educational needs. A need is anything that is a barrier to your child's ability to learn in a typical school setting. If the difference means your child needs something different from or additional to what is generally provided for other children of the same age, then it is classed as a special educational need.

This section usually starts with a summary, and then proceeds through each area of need, with a list of your child's strengths in this area, and their difficulties.

The four areas of development used in an EHCP are:

- Communication and interaction
- Cognition and learning
- Social, emotional, and mental health
- Sensory/physical

I explain more about special educational needs and what these categories mean in Chapter 2.

It is really important that your child's needs are accurate, and you are happy with how they are described. If your child's needs are downplayed, then your child won't have enough support. Similarly, if your child's needs are overplayed, then some schools might feel they can't cater for your child, or your child might have support which hinders their independence and development.

Examples of needs

Sensory and physical needs:

- Hattie has identified sensory processing difficulties. She finds high noise levels difficult, and finds smells such as the dinner hall or the school toilets very hard to tolerate.
- Marin has complex (whole body) cerebral palsy and is a wheelchair user. He cannot stand independently and his mobility and ability to complete everyday tasks is significantly affected. The condition also affects his speech – people who know him well can understand his speech patterns.

Cognition and learning:

- Nikki has a diagnosis of global developmental delay. At age five her development is around 18–24 months.
- Millie has a diagnosis of ADHD. For Millie this means she finds it very difficult to sit still and she can be very impulsive.
- Nadia finds writing painful and her handwriting is extremely slow and large.

Communication and interaction:

- Leon has a diagnosis of autism with a demand avoidance profile. For Leon this means he finds the ordinary demands and tasks of the classroom very difficult and anxiety provoking.
- Angelica uses limited verbal language. She communicates her needs through a mixture of single words, gestures, and Makaton signing.

Social, emotional, and mental health:

- Jessica finds the school environment extremely stressful and has had periods when she has not attended.

- Karl has a diagnosis of OCD (obsessive compulsive disorder). Karl engages in repetitive behaviours to help him feel safe, e.g. touching light switches repeatedly, washes his hands many times.

Section C – Health needs related to SEN

Section C is your child's health needs, related to their SEN or disability. Don't worry if there isn't anything in this section. The majority of health needs don't need to be included on an EHC plan. Health provision is agreed and managed by local health providers, and doesn't need to be part of their special educational needs. This also protects the confidentiality of your child and your family.

Children can also have an individual health plan, which is not related to an EHCP. You don't have to apply to the local authority for this, and the school can put this into place without additional funding. If your child has a lifelong condition such as diabetes, then this is the most appropriate way to support them.

Section D – Social care needs related to SEN

Section D is for social care needs. People are often scared of involvement from social services, but the job of social workers is to support families.

Social Care

Legally, as part of the EHCP process, social services have to be asked if there has been any involvement. This request does not mean any new process of investigation or assessment is being activated. If you have a social worker actively involved, they may be asked to give advice and comment on your child's strengths and difficulties. If you have had some involvement in the past, they may not record this information on the EHCP at all. You might have had involvement from organisations like CAFCASS (Children and Family Court Advisory and Support Service) if you have been through family court because of domestic abuse or another reason. You might also have had support from a social worker if your child is fostered, looked after, or adopted.

There are different teams in children's social work – child protection and disabilities. If you need support from social care, you can ask the local authority to assess your child's needs. You can also request an assessment of your own needs as a carer. If your child/young person is nearing the age of 18, you can request an assessment of what support they will need from adult social services.

Section E – Outcomes

Section E is for outcomes. Outcomes are like goals. Typically there will be a short-term outcome and a long-term outcome for each area your child is struggling with. It is common to set short-term outcomes to be achieved within a year, and long-term outcomes to be achieved by the end of the next key stage. Sometimes these outcomes are written collaboratively at a meeting with you, the coordinator and school, and maybe the EP. Sometimes they will be written by the EP when they write their assessment.

Outcomes

Outcomes work best when they are based on what you and your child want to work on, and start from your child's interests and strengths. They should draw on anything highlighted in Section A which you or your child want to work on or are concerned about. If your child has a particular interest, then one outcome could focus on ensuring that is developed and valued. If you are writing or amending outcomes, I would recommend starting from your child, and where they are right now, and thinking what is the next logical step for them.

Their purpose is to highlight what the provision (support) is aiming at – and to give a sense of what it is reasonable to expect your child to achieve, over the next year, and over the next key stage. In some contexts it is hard to set outcomes, as it's not clear what setting your child will go to, or we don't know how fast they will make progress, or your child might not yet be able to access the support offered. It is important to start from where your child is, and think about the progress they've made over the last year – this gives you a sense of what could be expected in the year going forwards.

It is common for outcomes to be given in a list near the beginning of the EHCP, perhaps like in this example.

UNDERSTANDING THE EHCP DOCUMENT

Outcomes
Cognition and learning
Long-term outcome: By the end of the next key stage, Charlie will be able to use whole-word reading approaches to read 10–20 high frequency words.
Short-term outcome: By the end of the year, Charlie will be able to read and write his name.
Communication and interaction
Long-term outcome: By the end of the next key stage, Charlie will be able to play a game with his peers in the playground with the support of an adult.
Short-term outcome: By the end of the year, Charlie will be able to take turns in a small group with the support of an adult.
Social, emotional, and mental health
Long-term outcome: By the end of the next key stage, Charlie will have a few peers he plays with consistently.
Short-term outcome: By the end of the year, Charlie will have a play date with a friend outside school.
Independence and self-care skills
Long-term outcome: By the end of the next key stage, Charlie will be able to take the bus to school on his own.
Short-term outcome: By the end of the year, Charlie will be able to walk to the corner shop to buy something on his own.

Section F – Special educational provision

This is perhaps the most important section of the EHCP, as it outlines what your child will receive in school or their educational setting. The educational psychologist will recommend the support and strategies they think your child needs in their assessment, and this usually forms the basis of Section F in the EHCP. The local authority is legally obliged to provide what is written in this section.

Each special educational need in Section B will have corresponding provision in Section F. Sometimes several needs can be met by the same provision, so it is okay for there to be some overlap or repetition in this section. Examples of provision are things like one-to-one support, an additional literacy programme, or special lunchtime arrangements. The provision in Section F must be specific and should normally be quantified. This means it specifies the number of hours, and how much a week, or month, or term will be available.

Section F – Provision
Nadia will be able to use a different entrance and exit to school to avoid the busy main entrance.
Nadia will be able to eat her lunch in an alternative, quieter location with a chosen friend.
Nadia will be able to opt out of singing assemblies and participate in an activity she enjoys in a quiet classroom.
Nadia will be met when she arrives at the school entrance by a consistent teaching assistant who she knows well.
Nadia will have twice weekly 30 minute sessions with a trained teaching assistant to follow an intervention to boost her reading skills, e.g. Toe by Toe or similar highly structured literacy interventions.

Preparation for adulthood

From Year 9 onwards, the following headings might be used, to focus on preparing for adulthood. This helps to focus on the future and plan for any support your young person might need in order to access and develop their independence. These are some of the things you might consider, but there is no prescribed list, and if the previous headings are still more relevant, they might be used as well.

Preparation for employment or higher education:

- Considering long-term goals for the future and breaking these down to work on over time
- Functional literacy and numeracy
- Support for finding and attending work experience placements
- Volunteering experiences in the world of work, e.g. animal shelters, community gardens, stables

Independent living:

- Life skills such as cooking, using a washing machine, managing a budget
- Independence, e.g. cooking, shopping, taking the bus, returning items to a shop
- Planning and organising trips

Friends, relationships, and community participation:

- Social opportunities which are outside the educational setting, e.g. community groups, sports groups, hobbies
- Volunteering opportunities
- Online safety

Health:

- Taking care of basic health needs
- Managing personal hygiene
- Booking and attending appointments

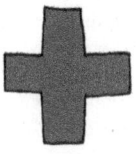
Health

What about health care – should that be in Section F?
This area can be complicated. It is now established that therapies which educate or train a child/young person should be included in Section F and may also be in Section G (health). This means occupational therapy, speech and language therapy, and sometimes talking therapies can be specified in Section F. A good question to ask to help determine whether the provision should be in Section F is, if my child didn't have this provision, would they still be able to receive education and/or training alongside the rest of the class? For example, your child might need specialist seating in order to be able to function in the classroom environment, and this should be in Section F, along with the arrangements for review and monitoring.

What does specified provision mean?
The SEN Code of Practice (DfE & DoH, 2015) states that provision in this section

> must be detailed and specific and should normally be quantified, for example, in terms of the type, hours and frequency of support and level of expertise.

The Code of Practice is clear that provision should be specified and quantified. This means the language should be specific about what is required: the hours, who will provide it, and their level of training should all be specified. There should be enough detail so you can tell what must be delivered, how often, for how long, and who by. Language such as 'might benefit from', 'access to', and 'opportunities for' doesn't give enough information about how the provision will happen and who will do it.

This is an example of specific language:

General language	Highly specified language
Mohammed will have weekly opportunities and regular support for developing his friendships.	Mohammed will attend the school nurture group one morning a week. Integrated into this session, he will have a 20 minute session with a trained teaching assistant and a peer. Activities should focus on developing his social interaction skills, including turn taking and listening to peers, and should include things which interest Mohammed, e.g. Minecraft, wild animals, physical activities.

It is usually the local authority educational psychologist's job to write the provision, and it can be very difficult to write good-quality highly specific provision, particularly if the school setting isn't yet decided, or if your child's needs vary.

Lia told me about her struggle to get all the support listed in her daughter's plan when she disagreed with school. Because what was written was open to interpretation, the school was able to argue for providing the support differently.

> The first EHCP, I thought, great, I've got it. I don't have to go to tribunal. I didn't understand that the wording wasn't good enough. Even though they had funding for a full-time one-to-one position, to cover somebody being with her at all times, for meals and breaks, and to cover training etc., that was being siphoned off, even though it was only a tiny school, for other people. The local authority said that's a problem for you and the school. When you've got somebody that's really anxious as a learner and needs a consistent person, you can't just chop and change who their support is based on the needs of your school. School were saying we're going to have a pool of TAs rather than allocating anybody

> specifically at the school. They said it was good for her, to get her less dependent on people.

Lia disagreed with how the school were providing support for her daughter, and wanted her to have a consistent adult. Children's needs can be met in a variety of ways, and there is not just one way of doing things. However, the advantage of highly specific, quantified support is that everyone knows exactly what should be happening. If there are problems, or the support isn't provided, you can refer back to the document for clarification and to argue for more support. If you end up going to appeal, or even a tribunal, a highly specified Section F means it is very clear whether it is being provided or not.

Section G – Health provision

This section describes any health care provision your child might need if they have learning difficulties or disabilities that affect their SEN. It can include any other health care provision reasonably required by a child or young person too, but does not have to. Any health care provision in Section G has to be agreed by the local commissioning body. This means that your local authority cannot include health care provision into an EHC plan without agreeing it with them.

If there are no health needs identified in Section C, then this section will be empty.

Section H1 and H2 – Social care provision

Social care provision can include support such as respite care, non-residential short breaks, practical assistance at home, home adaptations, or special equipment. These might also be provided through other branches of children's services, so may not be included fully here. Sections B and F are the legally enforceable sections, so most needs and provision within a normal day or provided via school should be included there.

Section H links to Section D. If there is nothing in Section D, there won't be anything in this section.

Section I – Placement
This is where the placement is named. This will be blank on your draft plan.

Section J – Personal budget arrangements
You have the right to request a personal budget connected to your child's EHCP, and it can be requested during the initial process or at an annual review. If your child is in an educational setting, this usually isn't something you need to worry about as the funds are delegated to them.

Personal Budget

A personal budget is an amount of money set by the local authority in order to deliver the provision outlined in an EHCP, which can be delegated to the parent to manage. It is usually relevant when the parent is involved in organising the provision, e.g. you recruit a one-to-one tutor or a personal care assistant at home, or you find and organise farm school provision once a week. A personal budget has to be used to support an outcome in the EHCP.

The funds can be held directly by the parent or young person or may be held and managed on their behalf by the local authority, school, college, or other organisation or individual and used to pay for the support specified in the EHCP.

Section K – Appendices
This is a list of all the reports and assessments which have been used to write the EHCP. Reports commissioned by the local authority and any you commissioned privately should be listed here. It doesn't need to include all the reports written about your child in their lifetime, as those which are most recent are most relevant.

EHCP examples
It is common for EHCPs to be presented like these examples. This makes it easy to see how your child's needs are linked to their support and outcomes. It is also easy to see, in the final column, how exactly it will happen, and who is responsible for organising and doing it.

UNDERSTANDING THE EHCP DOCUMENT

Section B Needs	Section E Outcomes	Section F Provision	Who will provide this? How often, when and where?
Mark has a significant language delay. He often does not respond to language used around him.	By the end of the year, Mark will be able to show joint attention with his teaching assistant for ten minutes. By the end of the key stage, Mark will be able to engage in a short, shared activity with a peer.	Structured activities which engage him based on his interests using Intensive Interaction strategies to encourage joint attention and shared engagement.	Daily in 5–10 minute bursts by the teaching assistant in the classroom, overseen by the teacher. The amount of time should increase as he is more able to pay attention.

Section B Needs	Section E Outcomes	Section F Provision	Who will provide this? How often, when and where?
Grace is not speaking in the classroom.	By the end of the year, Grace will feel able to talk to her mother about school and talking. By the end of the key stage, Grace will be happy to talk to her school friends.	Grace will have a learning mentor who spends time with her on a weekly basis, building a trusting relationship. Initially this should focus on activities Grace enjoys, including play or games outside to build her confidence. Over time, and at Grace's pace, it may also include writing or reading activities.	School support staff. A trained learning mentor with some additional training in Grace's difficulties with guidance from the SENCO. Weekly sessions of 45 minutes.

How to look at a draft plan

> Fatima got her EHCP by email with a formal letter from the local authority. She was alarmed to see she had only 15 days to respond, and it was the beginning of the school holidays, so she would have very little time to herself to do so. She didn't feel the needs in the plan reflected all of her child's difficulties, and it seemed like a few things had been left out from the reports she had read. She had already discussed them with the caseworker, but she couldn't see any changes in the document.

You need to be prepared for this stage, as you have 15 days to respond to the draft plan. In your response you should make any comments and request any changes you want and express your school preference. You can request extra time if you need, and you can also request a meeting with the local authority to discuss any changes you are requesting.

You must check a draft EHCP because it's a key document about your child. It will travel with them through their education and it describes what their needs are, and how school should support them. The school SENCO will use it to direct and inform what they plan for your child. School staff working with your child may not read all the background reports, so all the important information about their needs and their support must be in the EHCP.

It is much easier to change things when the plan is at a draft stage. The SEN caseworker will have read the reports and transferred the key information into the plan. Sometimes mistakes can happen in this process, or there might be small changes in the wording which can have a big impact on your child.

Reading your draft plan and the supporting reports is a time-consuming and daunting task, even if you understand all the language and jargon. It can have a significant emotional impact on you, and you might already be feeling very tired. You could ask someone else to read it as well, so you have another opinion, or there are organisations who will check your draft and reports for you, for a small fee.

UNDERSTANDING THE EHCP DOCUMENT

How will your child's day be different?

You can start by reading Section F through and imagining how that looks for your child's day. Think of their whole day – from when they arrive, to when they leave, different teachers and lessons, and how the suggested changes will influence that time.

School

Typical school day	What will be different – what is being offered
Arrival	Soft landing with TA
English lessons	One-to-one TA support
Break	
Maths lessons	Smaller group, recommended intervention
Lunchtime	Access to SEN hub

How will each need be supported?

Read the list of your child's strengths, and their difficulties (Section B). Do you immediately notice anything? If you do, make a note of it as it is easy to forget things when you are reading a long doc-

ument. You might want to make a table like this one, so you can see clearly what your child's difficulties are in school, and what provision is being suggested. Any gaps will quickly become obvious. You could also copy and paste things from the reports to make it easier.

Difficulty	How they will be supported
Difficulty understanding social rules	Social skills group, use of social stories
Misses instructions	All learning to be reinforced and repeated; adult support to start tasks
Not yet toilet trained	Intimate care plan, individual toileting plan; adult support to change as needed
Becomes overwhelmed by sensory stimuli	Quiet space within school; OT to provide programme of sensory activities to be delivered by teaching assistant
Difficulty managing transitions and changes to routine	Visual timetable; advanced warning of any changes

Checking a draft EHCP

Checking is important to make sure the EHCP is accurate and the recommendations made by the professionals have been incorporated into your child's plan. The EHCP is a legally binding document, and the local authority has to provide what is written in the plan. If at some point in the future, you have concerns about how your child is being supported, you can go back to the plan, and check that what is being provided fits within the legally binding provision. It will help you argue your case.

Before you start, get paper copies of the draft plan and the most important reports so you can see them in front of you. It is very hard to check a draft on a mobile phone. If you don't have a printer, printing shops will print documents for you from an email for a small fee, or you could ask your caseworker or school to give you paper copies.

Check the basics

- ☐ Can you see sections A through to J? The order and arrangement may be different and that's OK. There may not be information in all the sections.
- ☐ Check the personal information on the first page is correct.
- ☐ Read Section B. Do the needs include everything you would expect?
- ☐ Read Section F. Do you understand what support your child will get?

Do you have any concerns at this stage? Are there any changes you want to request? Questions you want to ask? Write them down straight away so you don't forget them.

Five steps to checking the content

Once you've checked the basics, you need to look at each of the professionals' reports, starting with the educational psychologist. This can take a bit of time and it will need concentration, so try and arrange some child-free time. You need to check that the needs and recommendations from the professionals' reports are represented in the draft EHCP.

1. Compare the educational psychologist's report with the EHCP.

   a. Look at your child's need/difficulties.

   Find the sections in the EP report where your child's needs are described. There is usually a list, and it will include your child's diagnoses if they have any. Compare the needs/difficulties identified in the EP report with Section B of the EHCP.

   b. Look at the recommended provision.

   Now compare the provision in the EP report, with the corresponding section in the EHCP, Section F (and G & H, if appropriate).

   c. Things to think about.

   If there are any differences, are you OK with the changes? Are there any significant changes of language between the reports? Highlight these to ask about. This is particularly relevant for provision, e.g. if the number of hours has changed from the EP report to the EHCP.

2. Check the other professionals' reports.

   You might have report from a speech and language therapist, or another specialist. Look at what they are recommending, and whether the recommendations are included in the EHCP. It isn't always easy to work out, as professionals may be recommending similar things, or a small recommendation may be part of a bigger point. You don't need points to be repeated, as it gets confusing to read.
   If there are any differences, are you OK with the changes?

3. Make a table (see below) which details any information that

is missing which you would like included, which report it is in, and where in the report it is located.

4. Make a list of any other issues you want to raise or questions you want to ask.

5. Send it back to the local authority.

Requesting additions or amendments

A table like this is helpful to make note of anything you want them to add to the final plan. You copy the information you want them to add, and record which report it is in, and where it is written. If you have lots of reports to look at it can quickly get confusing without a system like this.

Information to add	From the report	Where in report (in which section or page number and paragraph)
Copy the information you want added here	Speech and Language, 21.3.22	Receptive Language, page 2 paragraph 3

What happens next?

When you reply to the local authority, they might respond in the following ways:

- They issue a final plan with all the changes you want.
- They issue a final plan with some of the changes you want.
- They issue an unchanged final plan.
- They make some changes and send you another draft to look at.

If you and the local authority cannot reach an agreement it might be best to agree to have the final plan issued. Until you do this, you are unable to appeal. The issuing of the final plan triggers your right to appeal and mediation, which I will cover in Chapter 7.

UNDERSTANDING THE EHCP DOCUMENT

COFFEE TIME WITH ABI AND ELIZA

Eliza: One thing I was thinking that I've seen happen quite a lot is that families are getting very bogged down in wanting certain language. I would say bin all that. Just talk in a language that is suitable for everyone. The LAs are not going to be talking about monotropism and things like that. It's pointless. You're barking up the wrong tree. Just be plain speaking. Talk about the stuff they will know about.

Abi: People can get really stuck in conflict about using the language that they want in the assessment, right?

Eliza: Yes, like using a particular diagnosis like PDA or whatever. Just say they're very anxious and they will find direct demands are pressure. Use the descriptive terms. If the LA has a policy of not using the language, that's understandable. Don't get bogged down in trying to get them to understand all this stuff.

Abi: You don't need to. It just needs to be accurate about what your child is like. The other bit I wanted to mention is about how this stuff can be hard to read, and hard to relate to your child.

Eliza: Yes, I drew a cartoon about that. There they are having a lovely time playing on the swing, and having fun. And then, on the report, it says 'this child struggles to emotionally regulate', or 'finds it very difficult to concentrate for long periods' and needs 'highly bespoke education'.

Abi: It's tough to read. I really feel for parents when they are reading a draft EHCP.

CHAPTER 7

APPEALS AND TRIBUNALS

> Kirsty received her EHCP and was dismayed. The school her son Joe had been attending for the last year was named as his provision going forwards, despite all her efforts to demonstrate that he needed something more specialist. She knew she had to appeal but she wasn't sure how.

In this chapter I guide you through the appeals process, including mediation and going to tribunal.

If your EHC plan has been issued and you are happy with it, then you can skip to Chapter 8, which talks about what happens once you have a plan.

Is it worth appealing?

Appealing starts a formal disagreement process, which if it isn't resolved along the way, eventually goes before a judge in a hearing, where both sides get a chance to explain their argument.

Making an appeal is a legal process. Your rights to appeal are triggered at key decision points during the process. You can't just decide to appeal when you see what the council are planning to do, and you can't go to appeal before you get the decision letter that formally states their decision.

When you get a decision letter they will also send you:

- information on how to appeal if you want to
- information about mediation.

If you do appeal, the statistics are overwhelmingly in your favour. In 2021/2022, there were 11,000 appeals that went all the way through to tribunal, and parents and carers won 96% of those (Jemal & Kenley, 2023). Appeals don't have to go all the way to court and often it's possible to negotiate with the local authority, and a case can be resolved before it gets that far. The top three reasons for appeals are the contents of an EHCP, refusal to assess, and refusal to issue.

When can you appeal?

The process and possible points of disagreement (from Disabled Children's Partnership, Jemal and Kenley, 2023)

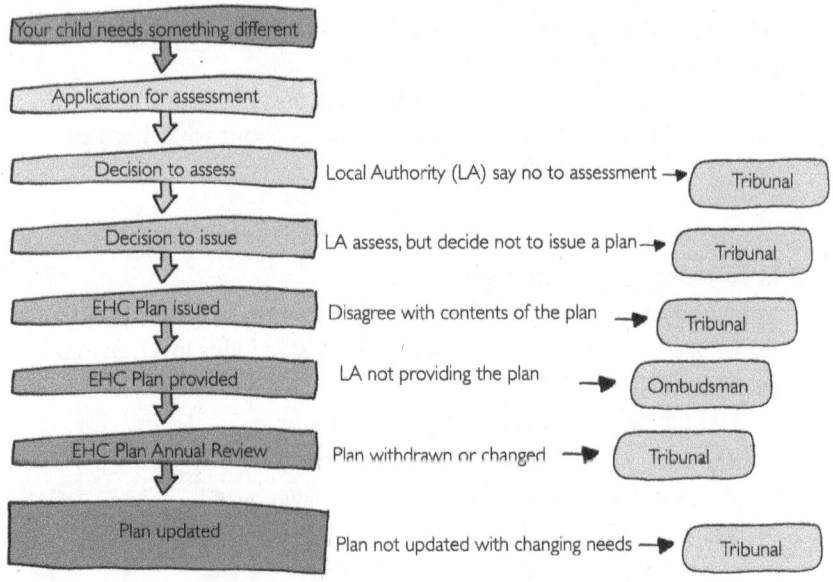

This is an outline of the EHCP process with the key steps and important decision points from the local authority highlighted. The diagram shows the key decision points, when the local authority might make a decision you disagree with. When you are at one of the points shown in the diagram, you are legally able to appeal to the SEND tribunal.

- Where are you at the moment in the ladder?
- What stage of the process are you at?
- There is no need to worry about the rest of the diagram – focus on where you are, and the next decision point.

Although the tribunal system was intended to be easy to navigate, lots of parents find it hard to find their way through the system. This is how Liane described it to me:

> It's supposed to be a system designed so that any parent can navigate it alone. I couldn't. I got help. I signed up to various advocacy services. I was constantly asking questions. It's because you're so emotionally invested in it. Reading case law when you're traumatised, trying to think straight and trying to think calmly and rationally and legally about something is incredibly hard.

Liane runs a support group for parents on Facebook and she told me about how she offers advice to parents who often have difficulties themselves, and who find it hard to keep track of the process, manage the paperwork, and know what to do. Other sources of advice and support for filling in forms can be school staff or SENDIAS. There are also a few charities that can help, some of which you will find under 'Useful Organisations' at the end of the book.

When can I appeal?

- The local authority decide not to assess your child. This is called a 'refusal to assess' appeal.
- The local authority decide not to issue an EHCP after doing the assessment.
- The local authority issue the EHCP but you disagree with what they've written – your child's needs or/and their provision. This is called a contents appeal.
- You disagree with the school they're suggesting on the EHCP.

- You have had an annual review and disagree with what the local authority decides to do.
- There are many more circumstances when you can appeal, but these are the most common.

This chapter will predominantly focus on refusal to assess and contents appeals, as this is what the vast majority of appeals and tribunals are about.

SEND Tribunal

When you challenge a local authority decision, it triggers an appeals process. If your issues aren't resolved during the process, it will culminate in a hearing in a special court called the SEND Tribunal. It is also called First Tier Tribunal or SENDIST, and it makes decisions that are legally binding. It's independent, national, and free to go to. It is a court of law, and focuses on what the law says, and what evidence there is for each argument. It hears parents and young people's appeals against local authority decisions about the special educational needs of children and young people.

The SEND Tribunal has the power to order local authorities to carry out needs assessments, issue plans, and amend existing plans. Tribunals are not about finding a compromise or negotiating a way forwards. The tribunal looks at the evidence that you put before it, both oral (spoken) and written, and decides whether the local authority followed the law and the code of practice. Local authorities have to comply with orders made by the tribunal.

The tribunal makes decisions based on what's right for the child at the date of the hearing, and based on the evidence it has in front of it. Parents can appeal decisions themselves, or can have support from an advocate, representative, or solicitor. Both sides of the disagreement, you and the local authority, submit evidence and you can bring expert witnesses who will be questioned.

Although tribunal is a formal court, they try to conduct hearings as informally as possible and to ask questions rather than taking an adversarial approach.

Legal language:

Appellant	The person who's appealing, so the parent or the young person.
Respondent	The local authority, they're responding to your appeal.
The bundle	All the paperwork for the hearing.
Lodged	Means registered.
The working document	A draft of the EHCP that goes between you and the local authority making amendments during the appeals process.
Grounds of appeal	The reasons for the appeal.
Paper hearing	The panel look at the paper evidence to make their decision – there will not be an in-person (physical or remote) hearing.
Court order	A direction issued by the court telling the local authority to do something.
Consent order	A legal document that confirms an agreement you're making with the local authority.
Case management directions	Information you get when your appeal has been lodged, which has the dates on it, and the timelines, and instructions, and witnesses.

You cannot go to tribunal when…

- you want more support for your child in school but they don't have an EHCP (and you haven't applied for an assessment)
- you have an EHCP but you're unhappy about how the school are supporting your child
- deadlines and timescales are not being met; you can report these things to tribunal if you currently have an appeal
- the local authority is not doing what the tribunal has told them to do; you can report this to the tribunal.

Mediation

Mediation is a less combative way of resolving disagreements than court. It involves all sides talking with a trained, independent mediator. It is quicker and less formal than a tribunal. You can take someone with you, and you can also ask professionals to attend with you and provide information to inform decisions. You can still go on to appeal to tribunal, even if you sign a mediation agreement.

When the local authority write to you and give you their decision, perhaps saying they won't assess your child, they will also send you details of mediation, and the timescales within which you have to respond. You don't have to go to mediation, but you do have to collect the certificate. There is a deadline of two months from the date of the local authority's decision letter to appeal. If you miss this date you can write to the tribunal and explain and request an extension.

Making an appeal

You are at a key decision point and receive a letter saying 'no' from the local authority. → Do you want to mediate?
- Yes → Reach agreement
- Yes → Don't reach agreement → Submit appeal
- No → Get letter from mediation service → Submit appeal

What is mediation?

Mediation sessions are with a trained, independent mediator who tries to help you reach agreement. They are impartial, they don't take sides, and they don't give advice. Their job is to manage the process and to help you communicate and explore the options for resolution. The mediator should be 'SEND accredited', indicating they have appropriate knowledge of SEND and the law and they will facilitate a balanced conversation, making sure everyone has a chance to speak, everyone listens to each other, and you can ask questions. All local authorities have a contract with an independent mediation service.

If you reach an agreement in the mediation meeting, the local authority has to carry out any actions that are in that agreement. The written mediation agreement is the only record of that meeting. If you only reach a partial agreement, you can still go on to appeal.

Mediation is voluntary. You don't have to do it before you appeal, and you can withdraw at any time. The mediation service will issue a certificate allowing you to appeal. The local authority must mediate with you if you ask for it. It's free of charge for parents.

If you've had a new report or a change in something since the EHCP was written and finalised, mediation can provide a chance to explain that. You may not have ever had the chance to sit down face to face with someone in the local authority. It can be a useful way to get an up-to-date understanding of the issues.

Are there any reasons not to mediate?

Mediation isn't always appropriate when there is a big imbalance of power. You might feel under pressure to make changes you don't really agree with, or you might feel like you should mediate because it's the 'right' thing to do, and would avoid expense on both sides.

Mediation can cause a delay in the process. You might have to wait for your mediation session. Sometimes it might be to your advantage to have some more time, if you want more time to prepare your appeal or gather evidence before going to tribunal. If a professional can't assess your child for another few months, it might be advantageous to you to have a delay. Likewise, it could also be used as a delaying tactic from the local authority.

I have heard stories about people getting stuck in mediation, having lots of meetings over time, but nothing actually shifting in the meeting and not making any progress. Several months or meetings can go by before you realise that they are not changing their position, and you are not changing yours. You cannot proceed to tribunal until you stop mediating. You might have to be the one to make that decision, as the local authority might not have a sense of urgency to resolve the case. The other thing to be aware of is that the local authority representative needs to be someone who has permission to make decisions on the spot. You can ask for the meeting to be rearranged with someone more senior attending if you know the person coming does not have the authority to make any decisions.

> Key points about mediation:
>
> - It's free and voluntary (for you, but compulsory for the LA if you want to).
> - You have to collect the certificate in order to appeal – this doesn't mean you have to go to mediation.
> - Whether you do or don't mediate makes no difference to how the tribunal views you and your case.
> - Be prepared to end mediation if nothing is changing.

Millie wanted to try and avoid a long tribunal process and chose to go to mediation when the local authority said no to conducting an assessment of her son.

> I started the EHCP process for my son. They declined to assess, and they said there's not enough evidence. I decided to try mediation as I wanted to resolve it quickly if I could, and I felt I did have the evidence. The meeting was really helpful – the caseworker listened and took everything very seriously. I pointed out the evidence I had, and I asked the school SENCO to come with me, which was really helpful as they added other things we hadn't thought of before. They agreed to assess and the process went smoothly after that – we got an EHCP.

Millie's experience of mediation was very positive. The local authority representative at the mediation meeting reversed the decision and her son was assessed and got an EHCP. Going to mediation saved her time and was a less stressful experience.

Appeals

Are you ready to lodge your appeal?
    Do you have your...

- ☐ decision letter from the local authority
- ☐ mediation certificate AND
- ☐ you are within the 2 month deadline?

How to submit your appeal

The forms for appeal are all easily available online. There are two forms for appeals. If the local authority have refused to assess your child, you need Form 35a. For all other appeals, you need Form 35. The forms go through a set of questions that you have to think about and you can also attach a document where you write more fully if you wish. There are videos on YouTube which take you step by step through how to complete the forms and explain what the questions actually mean.

The government have also published advice, 'How to appeal an SEN decision' (form SEND37), which you can download online.

You send in your form and the appeal is lodged, which means they register it.

What do I write on the form?

You need to know your reasons (grounds) for appealing and explain why you disagree with the local authority's decision. You have to say what you think needs to change, and give some reasons and the evidence you have. You don't have to use legal language in the appeal, but you need to give more explanation than just saying they have made the wrong decision.

You might have evidence of your child's attainment or perhaps lack of progress. You might provide examples of work or school reports or attainment results. You might have correspondence with professionals working with your child. You might have reports from educational or clinical psychologists, allied health professionals such as speech and language, occupational therapy, or medical professionals. You can refer in your appeal to any relevant legal issues.

Supporting evidence for an appeal checklist:

- ☐ School reports, meeting notes
- ☐ Letters and minutes from school or other professionals
- ☐ Educational psychologist report
- ☐ Speech and language therapist report
- ☐ Other professional reports
- ☐ Evidence of diagnosis, e.g. paediatrician letter, private report
- ☐ Annual reviews
- ☐ Written statements from people who work with your child, e.g. tutor, teacher

This is not an exhaustive list and you don't need them all!

The below story describes Ruth's experience:

> We started off just appealing on content, knowing that the reports would come. We put in some very vague appeal criteria and then we built our appeal as we went along. Midway through, we added Section I. Our hearing date was a year away, because at that point it took a year from when you lodged your appeal. But we were advised by SENDIAS that because it's a transition year we could use that and ask for it to be expedited because we needed the place for September. The local authority tried to block it but it was granted.

Appeals can take a long time to prepare. It will be read by the judge and will be discussed at the hearing, although it might be months away. As Ruth did above, you can submit a vague appeal, and then develop your argument over time, before the hearing. If your child is in a transition year, moving onto secondary school for example, you can get your case fast tracked, so the placement can be agreed in time for them to start their new school at the right time.

Refusal to assess appeals

'Refusal to assess' appeals are those at the very beginning of the process where the local authority decides your child does not need an assessment. Currently, 98% of these decisions are overturned in the favour of parents at tribunal. When the local authority is making its decision about whether to assess your child they will take into consideration things like what the school has done already, how they're supporting your child, and if they're making progress. But according to the law, the only thing that matters is the legal test. The SEND Tribunal will only apply the legal test and not your local authority's policy.

Typically the tribunal uses 'paper hearings' for this kind of hearing which means you submit the evidence to the tribunal and you waive the right to have the hearing in person and to have witnesses examined. Paper hearings are easier and quicker than in-person hearings. The tribunal distribute the bundle of evidence to the panel, they meet, and they issue their decision. You tick a box on the form to say you are happy for this to happen. Your case will be entirely based on your written submissions, so your evidence and how it fits with the law needs to be clear.

Refusal to assess appeals are usually half a day. Other appeals are a full day. If they need more time, the court will adjourn and set another date. Hearings usually start at 10 am in the morning or 2 pm in the afternoon. They all happen remotely (by video link), unless you specifically request an in-person hearing.

Contents appeals

If you are appealing about what's written in the educational sections (Section B, Section F, or Section I), this is called a contents appeal.

The EHCP should identify each need and it should include provision to meet each need. Section B is where your child's needs are identified and that should have specific and accurate information about each of those needs. Section F is the educational provision that will meet those needs. This is not dictated by what is available – so even if there isn't an appropriate school in your area, Section F should still say clearly what your child needs. If the appropriate provision isn't available, it doesn't affect what is written in the plan. If you're appealing on the school named (Section I), then it is usually sensible to appeal Sections B or F as well, because Sections B and F build the argument for Section I.

Extended appeals

Extended appeals are for children who have health and social care needs, as well as educational needs. An extended appeal allows parents to appeal all areas of their child's provision at the same time. This is called a 'single route of appeal'. The recommendations the tribunal makes for health and social care aren't legally binding. You can only appeal health and social care needs if you are also lodging an appeal about education.

At any point during the appeals process, you and the local authority can reach agreement with each other. This might happen at mediation, or when you've submitted your evidence. The local authority has a date by which it has to concede, if it is going to (their response date, in the case directions). If you don't reach agreement with each other, then the judge will look at the case and decide.

> Gill asked the local authority to assess her son Kye in Year 5 because she was concerned he would struggle with the transitions and multiple teachers he would encounter in secondary school. His primary school understood him really well and hadn't needed extra support to meet his needs. She had really struggled in secondary school herself and didn't want the same thing to happen to him. The local authority said no to an assessment, and she appealed their decision. She made an appointment with the local SENDIAS service to help her fill in the form. She decided not to mediate and began her journey to tribunal. She had evidence from a report from a speech and language therapist and reports from school, and a SENCO observation in class. When she got to tribunal the judge agreed with her that she had legal grounds for an assessment and ordered the local authority to assess Kye.

The appeal and tribunal process is often described using a 12-week timeline, from when you submit the appeal to the hearing date. Most parents I spoke to about their tribunal experience said their process took much longer than this. At the time of writing, parents commonly said their journey took a year, from appealing to having the hearing. If the council miss the deadlines, you can let the tribunal know so they are aware.

The tribunal will send you information, called 'case management directions':

> **Case management directions – important dates**
> - Date for you to submit information
> - Date for the local authority to respond to your information. The council has to respond to what you've said in your appeal. They can back down, or they might explain why they are fighting the case. Sometimes they quote the law in a general way, which is not particularly related to your case.
> - Date for submitting a witness list
> - Date for final submission of evidence

The tribunal timeline

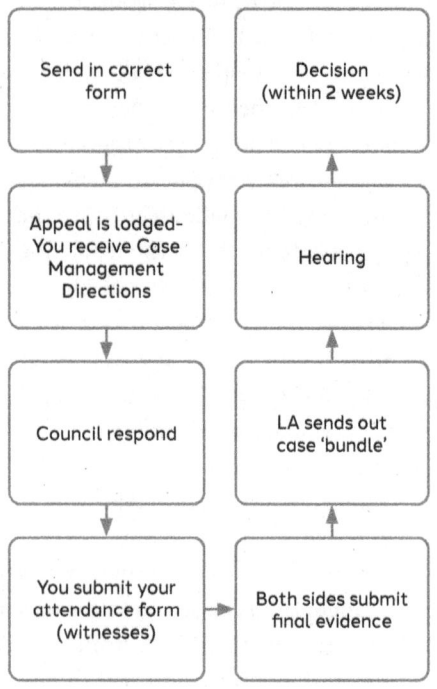

Do I need legal representation?

The short answer is no. You can represent yourself throughout the tribunal process. Most appeals are made without further representation, and part of the judge's job is to support you to be able to make your case. It is meant to be a system that parents can navigate on their own.

However, many of the parents I speak to talk about how hard it is to read case law and be calm and rational when it's about your own child. Whether you opt for representation depends on your situation, what you're asking for and your finances. Some parents get free support from people that they know who have some legal experience, who are able to read and research case law for them.

You can have a solicitor or a barrister represent you on the day. Barristers are more expensive, but they are skilled in arguing and take an adversarial approach. Solicitors can help you build a case and they can be at the tribunal as well. You can also have an SEN advocate present at the tribunal to help you. They can be at tribunal with you and speak for you, and they are not counted as a witness. They can take charge of the whole process, lodging the appeal and chasing it through to the hearing. They don't have legal training so they are cheaper, and they all have different experiences and training. Take care to check their qualifications and get recommendations from others if you can. Be wary of people who say they have very high success rates, or who sound too good to be true.

This is Elise's experience of trying to navigate the system on her own:

> Fighting for support through the tribunal system is daunting. You get this massive email. It says you're taking the LA to court. You must hit this timeline. You must hit that timeline. The support services are overwhelmed. The pressure is all on the parent. I run a parent peer-to-peer support group for neurodiverse children. The majority are parents who are neurodiverse. You have to learn how to navigate and work the system. I'm fortunate that I'm quite au fait with court

> procedure, law, and legal background from my own work. But because it's my own child, and it's myself, I find it really overwhelming and I just shut it away. Because it is so close to home, it is so hard for me to navigate. If it was somebody else's child, I could probably navigate it and not have an issue.

Do I need private reports?

Local authority decisions are commonly overturned at tribunal, with no legal representation necessary. This is particularly the case for refusal to assess appeals. You don't have to spend money to win an appeal. Look at your evidence and look at the law. In other circumstances, it depends what you're asking for and what evidence you have. Someone who is representing you at tribunal can only draw on the information you have so providing the evidence for them to use has to be your first priority.

If you are arguing for an independent school which is in a different local authority, then you are likely to need a strong case as this is an expensive option. If you're arguing that your child's needs are different to what the local authority says, and to what their EP says, you will need evidence to show that. Reports don't always have to come from external professionals, or be paid for. If your child has a tutor, they can write a report about how they are progressing and suggest what they need. If you've been to the GP to talk about their difficulties, they can write a letter.

Getting ready for a tribunal
Witnesses

The role of a witness is to provide factual evidence for the tribunal. The tribunal wants to hear from people who know your child well – it is useful to have people there who have worked with them over time in a relevant professional context. Witnesses need to make a written contribution in the form of a report or a statement, as well as attending in person. They are expected to attend the full hearing. You don't necessarily have to pay a witness.

You have to let the tribunal know they're coming in advance and explain what their role is. You will be sent the form for this in the case management directions. You are allowed up to three witnesses, but you do not have to have this many, and if you want more you can make a request. Legal support or advocates are not counted as witnesses.

Who could I bring as an expert witness?

- Teachers
- Specialist tutors
- Educational psychologists
- Other professionals
- Representative from the school you want, if the dispute is about school placement

What can expert witnesses do? They can just write a report, and not attend the tribunal. They can also do all of the following:

- Write a tribunal standard report
- Attend the hearing and be questioned
- Comment on the evidence of the other side
- Contribute to the working document
- Visit educational settings and comment on their suitability

Will went to tribunal for his son's education, as they felt he needed a specialist placement and the only option in their area was an independent school.

> We had to bring the local authority EP ourselves at our own expense because the local authority didn't bring him. It was great he was there because there was a lot of specificity to work out. The judge asked him a lot of questions about what he thought our son could manage and all those sorts of things. We got nearly everything we asked for.

This experience illustrates how useful it can be to have an expert witness there, if there are contentious issues. The judge at the tribunal asked the witness lots of questions about what he thought should be provided for Will's son, and this information fed into the plan and the provision the judge then agreed.

In some circumstances you might want someone to attend and they might feel unable to, perhaps they are a teacher and their school has said they can't attend. You can apply for a witness summons, where you make your argument saying why their evidence is important, explain why they can't come voluntarily and then the summons would be sent to you and you give it to your witness.

Your child can attend the hearing, but you need to plan for who will look after them whilst the court session continues. Typically, the tribunal will talk to the child at the beginning in a more informal way, or have a separate, informal conversation with them in another room.

Working document

If your appeal involves a challenge to the contents of the plan, then a working document will be produced by the local authority. It's a version of your child's plan, and it goes back and forth between you, with each side making amendments. It clarifies where the real areas of disagreement are and aims to reach as much agreement as possible before the hearing.

Bundle

The bundle is all the paperwork for the case, which is submitted as a whole to the tribunal. It will include reports, letters, statements, and evidence from both sides. They can be extremely long and cumbersome. There's written guidance from the tribunal about how they should be produced and different page number limits for different types of appeal, which are important to check in the tribunal guidance.

During the tribunal you will be expected to find your way round the document using the page numbers and paragraph numbers, and to use it to support things you say. Parents tell me they allocate significant time to going through the bundle, and adding tabs, markers and highlights so they can find the most important information quickly.

Reaching agreement before the hearing

Cases can always be settled in advance of the hearing by agreement. This can happen right up to the last minute. If the local authority decide not to oppose your appeal, then the appeal is decided in your favour, and it can be closed. If this happens, you should ensure you have the decision in writing before you withdraw your appeal. Alternatively the tribunal can issue a consent order. Make sure you have it in writing before you agree anything, and you should have a signed copy of the amended EHCP if it's a contents appeal.

What happens at a tribunal?
Who is there?

The judge and one other person will look at the evidence and decide what the key issues are. They read all of the information and ask questions of the witnesses present. One panel member will always be the judge and they will be a lawyer, a solicitor or a barrister. Their role is to ask questions and to ensure that the hearing is conducted fairly and justly. They also have to make sure that the decision that's reached is lawful, and they draft the final decision.

The other panel members, or member, are the specialist members and they are chosen because of their expertise and experience in SEN. They are at the hearing to ask questions and to help the tribunal in its understanding of particular issues relating to SEN. They're not a solicitor or a barrister.

The clerk will come online with you beforehand to check you understand how it's going to work and go through anything that has been agreed or submitted at the last minute, such as late evidence or final working document changes.

What happens at a hearing?

Every hearing is different, and the tribunal panel approaches cases individually. Hearings usually start with the judge doing an introduction, explaining the tribunal procedures and listing the issues to be considered. Sometimes they ask you to talk a little about your child and the current situation. Then they will go through the appeal one issue at a time. You and the local authority will have a chance to give your views and present your evidence on each issue. You have the chance to ask questions of the local authority and their witnesses and you have the chance to add anything else that you feel is important that hasn't been mentioned. The council are given the same opportunity though they don't usually question you personally. At the end, you might be invited to make a brief closing comment to summarise your position.

You will need to refer to the 'bundle' all the time. If you are using an electronic version, you will need it on a separate device. As they speak or ask questions, people will give page numbers and paragraph numbers and expect you to be able to find the information that they're talking about.

Sometimes people submit video recordings of their child and this can be a helpful way to ground the discussion in reality, and make it more personal. This might be a helpful thing to do if you feel that their needs aren't adequately described, as making a short video can in some circumstances help the tribunal to understand the issues better.

This is Rick's story about going to tribunal:

Everything had been leading up to this day for months. It was incredibly tense. I couldn't sleep for about a week beforehand. I knew our whole case inside out. I could remember everything that happened in encyclopaedic detail. I kept worrying about things I'd left out or forgotten to do.

I couldn't think beyond the hearing date. We were on tenterhooks up until the last minute. It seemed like the LA might settle. They really didn't have much of a case, but they didn't. Our hearing was online, which felt weird. I was just sat as usual on the sofa. I did dress up, which helped me get in the right frame of mind.

And it was lucky because they were all in suits. It was absolutely exhausting. It lasted all day and you have to follow what's going on and concentrate the whole time. We had a massive bundle of paper and people gave out the numbers of the pages and the paragraphs they were referring to.

Questions to consider:

- What is the relevant law?
- What evidence is there that supports what I want?
- What evidence is there that goes against it?
- What's the local authority position?
- What are the weaknesses in their case?
- What are the weaknesses in my case?

Tips for remote hearings:

- Think about where you are going to be.
- Minimise distractions, e.g. from children in the house.
- Dress as though you were going to court in person.
- Put your phone on silent.
- Make sure you can easily access the 'bundle'.

- Tell the judge if something is happening at home which is distracting you – this cannot always be avoided, but they won't know unless you say.
- They will not know you have a problem unless you tell them, e.g. if you need a break.

When do we know the decision?
You don't normally hear the decision on the day. The panel go away and consider all the evidence. They will take what's written and what's been said into account and then make their decision in writing. This can take two or three weeks. Regardless of whether they decide in your favour or not, there are timescales prescribing what happens next, which are usually requirements on the local authority to carry out the decisions that have been made.

Disagreeing with the tribunal
If you think that the decision that they've made is wrong, or that there's another reason why you want the tribunal to look again at the decision, you can ask for them to review it, and you can ask for permission to appeal. You ask the first tribunal for permission, and then take your case to the upper tribunal. The upper tribunal is where case law is made. Case law is binding on later cases, and makes clear how the law is going to be applied.

There are other places that you can go to to complain. They have their own particular procedures and situations. The Local Government Ombudsman is for complaints about the local authority. Judicial review is an option in specific circumstances, and you would need legal advice to pursue that process. If your complaint is about the local authority, you can also follow their complaints procedures.

The emotional impact of tribunals
Hoppy told me about her experience in the appeals process and the shift change she felt in her relationship with the local authority. She describes how she developed a way of being and a way of relating to them which helped her cope during the process.

APPEALS AND TRIBUNALS

> Once we got into tribunal, it felt like there was a line drawn in the sand. We are now against you. We are not trying to help you. When I'm speaking to the local authority, I speak like a lawyer. It's extremely polite, but factual with no emotion in it. I was not like that in the early days. You start off as this emotional person trying to get people to see your point of view, and then you realise it's futile. You grow a set of armour and treat it like a job. I have learned to not be emotional to people who do not care.

Taking care of yourself in the process:

- Learn to speak like a lawyer.
- Develop your armour – your protective skin.
- Protect your time off – don't answer the phone or check emails.
- Find others who are going through the same thing – both locally and online.

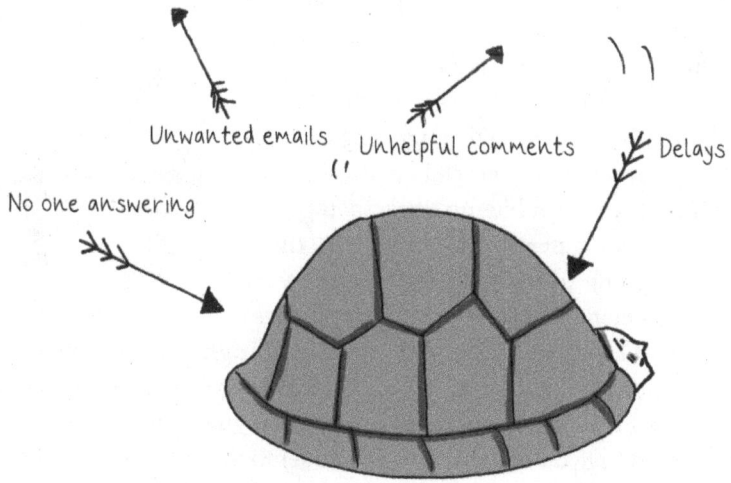

Do I need legal representation?

The tribunal system is set up for parents to navigate on their own. You don't usually need legal representation. You can go to tribunal (and most parents do) without a solicitor or barrister. Getting legal help can be very expensive but if your case is complicated, or the financial stakes are very high (perhaps you want them to go to an independent specialist school) then you might be thinking about representation. There are specialists in SEN law who will be able to advise you about your case and structure your arguments and help you gather evidence. The local authority would then direct all their communications to them, and perhaps involve their own legal team.

What about advocates?

Advocates are people who you pay to offer you advice and guidance. They can be the main point of contact for the local authority, and handle all communications. They are a lot cheaper than having a solicitor involved. They are unregulated, and have different experience and qualifications. It's best to get a recommendation if you can, and look for someone with lots of experience. Be aware that they charge differently – sometimes by the month, sometimes by task. If your case turns out to be prolonged, it is generally better to pay by task, e.g. per email.

COFFEE TIME WITH ABI AND ELIZA

Abi: I think it feels really hard to disagree with the local authority, and potentially you're also disagreeing with the school that your child is at.

Eliza: It can feel like no one's seeing your child's needs. And of course, that's going to feel very difficult and very emotional. It can be very scary because it's very official, isn't it? And really frightening that potentially where you're at now, that you're going to have to be in this kind of world. And often it's language that isn't something you're used to or can understand easily as well. It's a very different way of communicating.

Abi: The letters are legal and they can feel quite threatening, even though they're entirely generic, they're sending out the same letters to everyone.

Eliza: You're sitting there as someone full of emotion, dealing with things that are not emotional and are not going to reference your emotional distress. If you're prepared for that and you understand how this system works, it can be helpful just to know that they are not going to say 'this must be very stressful for you'. They're not going to be at all kind.

Abi: They're just going to be professional, they're going to hold you at arm's length.

Eliza: Also, I think this is a thing that is done everywhere, local authorities and councils have a 'no' as their first response. They have to do a 'no' first and then deal with those who come back. Even before you get to an appeal, it's worth noting that the panel may very well turn you down the first time. You can ask to be put back in and say that you will continue to be put back into panel every week. Often that leads to a massive shift and then you don't need to go to an appeal. Telling them I'm not going to give up.

Eliza: It's always evidence and fact based. If you are going to tribunal to get a setting, it will be based on the fact that other settings are not suitable. You will need your evidence to that. It's not about you saying, I prefer that setting.

I suppose it's helpful to understand that this is going to be an incredibly protracted process in a difficult system, perhaps even seeing it like buying a house where it's going to take ages and it's going to be seemingly very slow. And whilst you don't want to take your foot off the pedal, and you do need to keep track of dates and deadlines, you also need to find a way to shut off from it.

Abi: I really like that analogy of the house buying because it is like buying a house, but over maybe 18 months.

Eliza: And reiterating to yourself that this isn't an emotional issue for them, whilst our emotions can feel very heightened, this isn't going to impact the outcome positively, it's not going to make any difference. Sometimes we can get quite emotional when we speak to these people and then that can feel quite horrible, that we've kind of had that turmoil with people who are not listening and not caring. If you do get either really angry or really upset it's not going to make success any more likely and it might make the relationship more difficult.

CHAPTER 8

ANNUAL REVIEWS AND TROUBLESHOOTING

Rathika's son Eshan had finally got his EHCP and she was very relieved he had all the support she thought he needed and she felt really hopeful this would be a fresh start for him. She really needed a rest and was looking forward to a break. But when he started at his new school, it didn't all go well immediately, and they were still struggling to support him. They found it hard to recruit someone to work with him and didn't yet have all the sensory equipment specified in the plan. She found that although he had the EHCP, it wasn't always easy for school to provide the support, even though they had good intentions.

We have the EHCP. What now?
This chapter is about the annual review process, and some common problems some parents face once their child has an EHCP.
Your child finally has their EHCP and you've worked hard on it. You really need a rest from it all – but you can't just sit back and relax. Maintaining the plan and making sure the provision is in place needs attention and energy. It is wise to keep an eye on the provision in school, and to remain aware of potential issues so you can act early.
When a school agrees for your child to attend there, they will have seen the EHCP and agreed they can meet their needs. This means they agree that they can put in place the provision which is listed on the plan. Sometimes this all goes according to plan, and the provision is put in place and things get better. Sometimes there are issues around implementing the recommended provision – often these issues are around funding, staff recruitment, and transitions.

The main way in which EHCPs are monitored and reviewed is through the annual review process. As your child develops, the needs, provision and outcomes will likely need to change as they grow up. This process of review is a legal process, with a timeline and fixed requirements.

Annual reviews

When your child has an EHCP, you will have an annual statutory meeting with school, called an annual review. This is a legal process which looks at the needs, provision, and outcomes specified in your child's EHCP Education, Health and Care Plan and checks they are accurate, and agrees any changes that are needed.

The structure and requirements of the annual review are stipulated in the Children and Families Act (2014) and in the SEN Code of Practice (DfE & DoH, 2015). If the legal process isn't followed, you can refer them to the law, and demand that it is followed, and ask for the meeting to be delayed. It is an eight-week

process which includes asking professionals their views, asking you and your child, and making amendments. It's the local authority's responsibility for the process to happen, but this is usually delegated to the school/educational setting who will host the meeting if your child is in school. Whoever hosts the meeting will write to everyone involved to ask their views. In most cases this is the school SENCO.

Annual reviews focus on the child/young person, and the progress they're making. The meeting will ask if the provision, including the placement and the support, is still suitable. There might need to be new outcomes written if they've been achieved, and a review of the provision as your child develops and grows up. Sometimes it might ask if your child still needs an EHCP, or if it should be ended. It should be a chance for you to say what you think, your child to express their views, and the professionals who are working with them to update their recommendations.

What is an annual review for?

- Time to focus on your child/young person
- Talk about the progress they are making
- Review the provision – is it still appropriate?
- Look at the needs, the provision, and the outcomes
- Find out what you think, and what your child thinks
- Find out what the professionals think

Who should be there?

- Your child (at some point, or be represented in another way)
- Head/SENCO
- Someone from the LA SEN department
- Other professionals as depends on your child's needs and circumstances: health professional, speech and language therapist, occupational therapist, teaching assistant

Your child can come at some point, either just to say hello, or if they are able to, sit in on part of the meeting. One parent told me she had videos of her son to show at the annual review and that for her that felt like the most important thing because it made his progress and how he was doing really central to the meeting, although he wasn't able to attend.

The headteacher or SENCO of the school will be there and someone from the local authority SEN department should be there. The attendance of other professionals depends on your child's needs and circumstances. The local authority educational psychologist is usually invited but in my experience does not have the capacity to attend. Other professionals such as a speech and language therapist, occupational therapist, or teaching assistant might come, depending on what your child's needs are.

Parents often say to me they don't feel like they had a meaningful input in meetings – the parent role is often to agree, not to question. There is a power imbalance when professionals work with families. In meetings and reports parents are often referred to by their first name, or even by their roles 'Mum' and 'Dad'. Parents often report feeling blamed and dismissed and feeling that they can't win. You might also experience what many parents do: they start to feel like children again in the school context, with teachers 'telling them off' if their child isn't coming into school or doing their homework. You might be worried about being judged or fearful that social services might be called if you are honest about how difficult things are.

In case it needs saying, there is no 'parent role' that you have to fit into – you can contribute as much or as little as you want to, you can ask questions, write things down, invite people along to support you. The meetings are for parents, as much as anyone else.

One way of approaching the meetings is to develop a role for yourself, as a 'professional parent'. You could think about what you can do to feel as confident as possible in the meeting, and how you can feel the equal of the professionals there. Parents tell me it helps if they understand the jobs of the people present, and if they are clear on what the purpose is for the meeting. They dress and present themselves as if they are going to work, rather than doing the school run. They arrive a little early, so they feel calm, and have time to say hello to everyone there. Some people like to take notes, so they know they have the important things on record.

What is a 'professional parent'?

- Smart clothing
- General appearance, e.g. hair, make up, jewellery
- Know everyone's name and role and make sure they know yours
- Go with some written things you want to say
- Arrive early
- Ask if important points have been minuted
- Don't take mistakes personally

Marianne's daughter is 16 and she has been going to annual reviews for her since she got a plan aged five. She has developed the concept of being a professional parent, which she uses to help her keep a calm, detached air in meetings. She makes sure everyone knows her name and isn't calling her Mum. She makes sure she knows their names and their roles as well. She puts key dates in her diary for the process so she can follow up quickly if it's not started. She doesn't take it personally if she doesn't get an invitation or a document. She writes it off as an admin error, because she is seeing this as a job.

She doesn't like annual reviews, and she finds them intimidating and sometimes a waste of time, but reframing it so she sees it as her job as a parent has really helped. Thinking of herself as a professional parent helps her express herself politely but firmly and assertively, and to take on a different persona.

She knows as much about the process as any of the professionals there, and she does things like making sure someone is taking minutes, because she's learned from experience that having those important decisions recorded prevents problems further down the line. She's decided that the most important things for her in that meeting are Sections B and F, needs and provision, and she asks that they're discussed first, because she's realised that quite often the professionals have to leave after an hour, and then if you haven't got to B and F yet, then they've missed that. She knows she wants their input on those sections. She asks school to start with those bits. She goes to meetings with an idea of what she wants, and she says she knows she's more likely to be listened to if she acts with school, so she always tries to work with them.

The actual meeting is part of a broader process which takes eight weeks. Four weeks in advance of the meeting, the school will send out invitations and a request for information, to you and other professionals involved. Two weeks after that, those reports should be circulated amongst everyone that's coming to the meeting. Then the meeting happens, and two weeks after that, the school should send out the report, and make recommendations on any amendments. Two weeks after that, the local authority will make a decision. They can choose either to amend the plan, not to amend the plan, or to cease the plan. You then have 15 days to respond to that decision.

ANNUAL REVIEWS AND TROUBLESHOOTING

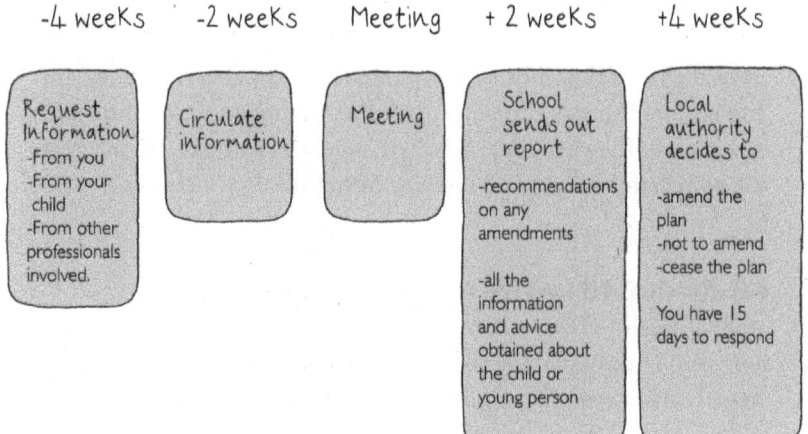

The legal requirements for an annual review:

- You are asked for your views.
- Your child is asked to make a contribution.
- Professionals are asked to write reports.
- This information is circulated in advance of the meeting.
- The meeting date is the anniversary of when the EHCP was issued, or the last annual review.

Things to look out for:

- Put an approximate date when you expect the meeting in your diary (the anniversary of the last meeting, or if this is your first annual review, the anniversary of the date of issue of the EHCP).
- Mark the date four weeks in advance of this, when you expect to receive an invitation to the meeting.
- Mark two weeks in advance, when you expect to receive reports to read.
- After the annual review, look out for the local authority decision about whether they are going to make any changes, which should be within four weeks.

- There is no statutory date for sending you a copy of the newly amended plan.

Even if the local authority hasn't held an annual review, they are still required to write to you to say they are maintaining the plan, or whatever they have decided. That should be within 12 months of the plan being made or 12 months from the last review.

What should I write in my contribution?

You will need to write a contribution in advance, and perhaps support your child in making their contribution. This is also something school can do, and they often have a standard form they use.

The local authority might give you a form to use to write your contribution; you are also always free to write your own contribution. Take some time to think about what's happened in the past year, what progress your child has made since the last annual review. You might want to consider what could have gone better over the past year, and then think ahead about the priorities for your child in the year ahead.

- What has worked well for your child in the past year?
- How has your child progressed since the last annual review?
- Looking back over this year, what could have gone better?
- What's important for your child in this year coming up – both from their perspective, and from yours?
- Is there anything else you would like to discuss at the meeting?

This is what Michal wrote for his daughter's annual review:

> This year has been up and down for Eliana. She found the transition to Year 8 and a new teaching assistant difficult. She is still very anxious at school and it is still sometimes hard to get her through the door. She says she doesn't have any friends and the work is too hard. She particularly doesn't like her Maths lessons and PE lessons and it is harder to get her into school on those days. She has been having difficulty sleeping throughout the year and wakes up a lot

which affects all of us. The needs in the EHCP seem a bit out of date as they are from Year 4. Now she is in secondary school things have changed a lot. I think she is going to need more tailored support or she is going to struggle more academically. She is finding it hard to organise herself for homework and what she needs at school. Going into Year 9, we are worried about how she will cope as they start to look towards GCSEs. Eliana loves dance and drama, and we would like to have more chances to do these at school. It would be great if she could use her laptop at school, as writing is painful for her and it means she writes less than she can. It would be good if she had somewhere to go at lunchtimes as she says she is often on her own, and isn't happy about this.

How do I make amendments to the EHCP?

Most amendments can be made with school at the meeting fairly easily. If you want to make significant amendments, which might require changes in funding for example, you might need more evidence or a reassessment.

> Tips for making amendments:
>
> - Is there evidence that their needs have changed or aren't being met?
> - Agree changes needed with school.
> - Make concrete suggestions of things you think will help if you can.
> - You or school should make the amendments clearly on the document.
> - You might need a pre-meeting or a post-meeting to discuss and clarify points after the main annual review.

If you want to make amendments to your child's provision which will require additional funding it is likely to be particularly important to have updated reports and information from the professionals working with your child. The provision which is expensive is that which requires people's time – so more time with a teaching assistant, or more allocated sessions with a professional like a speech and language therapist. You might want to have discussions with those professionals, and develop a shared understanding of the issues. If the reports aren't ready in time for the annual review, you can ask for the annual review to be delayed. If there's new information in the reports then that will be particularly important.

It's always better to work with the school if you can, because if they agree with you, you have a stronger voice. Evidence from several people is always better than just one. I know one local authority whose annual review process includes two additional meetings, one before and one afterwards, as they find there is too much to cover in one meeting. This also has the advantage of keeping each meeting relatively short, rather than one very long discussion.

Professionals commonly come to part of an annual review, but are not able to stay for all of it. It is worth asking if any problem solving or discussion about changing needs happens when they are present, as their input and perspective could be very influential and helpful. This often means focusing on Sections B and F first, as this is where they have most input.

Take notes of the amendments that you want, as it's much easier to have a discussion if there's something concrete to start from. You could look at the current EHCP and highlight sections which are out of date, or write some suggestions.

Phase transfer reviews

This is the term used to describe the meeting when a child is moving from one phase of education to another – moving from primary to secondary school would be the most obvious example. Children with EHCPs are given extra consideration at these times, to ensure they have a suitable placement named well in advance and the transition can be well managed. It is helpful for these meetings to be scheduled in October/November in order for the whole process to be finished in time, and allowing for any delays in the process. There are legally mandated dates by which you should have the next setting named. These are listed below.

ANNUAL REVIEWS AND TROUBLESHOOTING

> **Dates for phase transfer meetings**
>
> Date you should receive the amended EHCP, naming the next setting by:
>
> - 31 March
>   - Starting school
>   - Post-16 transfer (or five months before transfer takes place)
>
> - 15 February
>   - Infants to juniors
>   - Middle school to high school
>   - Primary school to secondary school

Early annual reviews

If you have significant concerns and your child is really struggling, it is important to meet with the school as soon as possible. Don't wait for the next annual review to discuss problems.

Early annual reviews might also be called interim or emergency reviews. They can be held at any time, so one scenario might be if your child is at risk of exclusion. In that event, the school can arrange the review, or you can ask the local authority to arrange one. There isn't a legal duty on the school to comply with your request, and having an early annual review is at the discretion of the local authority. If you want one, it will help if you can get the school's support. If they suggest having a normal meeting, rather than an annual review, it is worth considering whether you want or need the legal protections which an annual review gives you. If the meeting is run as an annual review it triggers the right to appeal (Chapter 7) if you disagree with the outcome.

If you feel that you need an up-to-date assessment because the EHCP just isn't right anymore, you might need some evidence to back that up. Local authority educational psychologist time is under considerable pressure so you would need to construct an argument as to why this is necessary.

Preparation for adulthood

Preparation for adulthood is for all children from Year 9 upwards. It provides some ideas to think about the options and choices for your child's next phase of education or training. You can find more ideas about what might be relevant in Chapter 5. There are four subcategories (Education and employment, Independent living, Maintaining good health, and Friends, family, and community), which might be used instead of, or in addition to the Section B categories.

Preparation for adulthood is a way to ensure the right services are mobilised and the supports which school or college could offer to help develop your child's independence are put in place. It might mean starting to have conversations about work and career interests, or thinking about a vocational profile. Sometimes it means considering what additional support your young person needs in order to access work experience, or other ways to support them to get experience in the world of work or volunteering. Sometimes outcomes might begin to focus on developing independent living skills, such as budgeting, shopping, or independent travel. The purpose is to think about how young people can have as much choice, control, and freedom over their lives as they can.

The emotional impact of meetings

Sometimes annual reviews are stressful. They can bring up memories of previous, difficult meetings or they can remind you of being at school yourself.

> Mila was worried about her 14-year-old son's annual review. He had been suspended from school a few times, and she was concerned school might say they couldn't keep him, or blame her for his behaviour. She felt some of his teachers were not managing him very well but was scared to mention this for fear of sounding critical of the school. She thought in advance about what she wanted to say and chose her words to avoid sounding critical. She practised saying it to a friend. She started off the meeting by saying her piece, to get it out the way. She was taken by surprise when the SENCO said it wasn't just her son that was struggling in those lessons, and she didn't think it was his

fault. The SENCO said she thought her son was making great progress in some subjects and gave some examples which made Mila feel extremely relieved. The SENCO suggested putting him in a different group for science and maths with different teachers, which Mila was happy to do.

Mila found that the meeting was easier than she expected, and writing down what she wanted to say in advance helped. Another approach could be to send an email in advance, or to take someone supportive with you.

Discussions about your child can evoke strong emotions, and it can help to prepare what you want to say and to take some time for yourself afterwards.

Tips for saying difficult things:

- Practise saying what you want to say at home.
- Write down the important things you want to say, sometimes it helps to write it word for word, like a script.
- Take someone else with you for support.
- Get a staff member who knows you and your child well to come.
- Take notes in with you.
- Talk to someone in school in advance about your concerns.

Things to help process your feelings:

- Release the anger and frustration, e.g. writing a letter, visualise blowing everyone up, visualise the person who said the most difficult thing turning into a slug. It is all in your head, and won't harm anyone, but it might help you feel better.
- Block in some time to relax afterwards – don't go straight back into work or childcare.
- Think about how to connect with your child in a positive way – bring their strengths to mind, do something to connect with them that you both enjoy.

- If you are left with some thoughts which are hard to let go of, you could imagine them as rocks, and throw them against the wall, or drop them down a well, or pack them up in a box.

They aren't getting the support stated in the EHCP

If the provision in your child's EHCP is not being provided, I wouldn't wait for the annual review. What you want to change isn't what's written in the document, but what's happening on the ground in the classroom. Depending on your child's setting, it's usually best to start by talking to the teacher and then work your way up the hierarchy in the school. I would be as specific as you can about what you're worried about. If you don't feel you are being heard, you might need to put your concerns  in writing, and put a date in the diary to meet again, to see if things have improved.

Hatty, who I worked with, described her approach to me as being 'stealthy persistence'. She tried to maintain a good working relationship with school staff, by consciously deciding not to blame the individuals concerned. She then gently, but continually, reminded them of the issues that needed to be resolved, and kept arranging chances to talk about it, and let them know she would check in again to see how it was going.

Staff recruitment

Recruiting staff to fill one-to-one positions to work with children can be difficult. Sometimes it is stated on the EHCP that staff who work with the child must have specific training in a particular approach. In my experience, going on a specific training doesn't mean a teaching assistant will be able to build a relationship with your child. Children need staff who relate to them as individuals, get to know them well and are responsive and flexible. In schools I have worked in, the headteacher knows which teaching assistants are naturally responsive and understand children's differences and what they need in an intuitive way. Schools will often place these assistants with the children where they are most needed, when they are able to.

Funding

Funding is determined by the local authority in collaboration with the school, so you don't have to be involved or worry about the detail. Each local authority will have its own mechanism for allocating funding associated with EHCPs, and the way that funding from local authorities works can change, according to decisions from national and local government, as well as policy changes. Educational settings receive money in their normal budgets to support children with SEND. Settings are expected to fund the initial support for children with additional needs from their already existing budget. This money is not ring-fenced for SEN, so can be spent on other things. Top-up funding (sometimes called 'element 3') funding is only available when your child has an EHCP. Local authorities give this money to schools. The amount is related to the level of need specified in the EHCP, and local authorities may use banding as a way to categorise how much additional financial support your child will receive. If your local authority uses banding, it should be determined after the provision has been agreed. It cannot be used instead of specifying provision. The local authority is responsible for providing the support, if the school is not able or willing to do so. Legally, under Section 42 of the Children and Families Act (2014), the local authority must provide all the special educational provision in the EHCP.

Transitions

A transition is any change point – so when your child starts school, when they change teacher in primary school, and when they move to middle school or secondary school. Transitions often involve lots of change, and there is the potential for things to go wrong. It is always worth checking that the information about their SEN has been transferred and read by the new teacher, or the appropriate staff. You might want to schedule a meeting near the beginning of the new school year in September to talk about what's needed and to discuss any queries. This is a good way to ensure that busy school staff have time to read the EHCP and consider what your child's needs are. What the EHCP says isn't always immediately comprehensible, so it is a chance to talk about what it means in practice, and to discuss how that will look in the new setting or classroom. It is much better to meet new staff and get to know them before there are any issues, or else your first proper meeting might be when something difficult has happened.

Mark talks here about his daughter Mel's experience during the transition from primary to secondary school.

> When Mel moved from primary to secondary school I knew it might be a bumpy transition. She didn't have an EHCP, but she did have a lot of assessments and she was receiving quite a bit of one-to-one support. Somehow the paperwork never got to the right person, though it was never clear where the communication problem had happened. I had assumed school knew what to do. But when I finally spoke to the Head of Year in March that year, when she'd started in September, she didn't know Mel had any special needs or had had any additional support in primary school. Once I explained that she had dyslexia and dyspraxia and needed adaptations like not being expected to copy anything from the board, coloured overlays, reduced writing requirements, and shorter homework, she sent the information round all her teachers, and things got a lot better after that.

As this story highlights, information can be mislaid during transitions but often it can be sorted out quite easily.

Problem corner
When will the EHCP stop?
The SEN Code of Practice (DfE & DoH, 2015) says that local authorities must not cease to maintain the EHC plan simply because the young person is aged 19 or over, but there are some clear times when a plan should end:

- A young person aged 16 or over leaves education to take up paid employment (including employment with training but excluding apprenticeships).
- The young person enters higher education.
- A young person aged 18 or over leaves education and no longer wishes to engage in further learning.
- The young person turns 25.

What if we disagree?
If you disagree with what the local authority is suggesting, you have the right to appeal. The same appeals process applies to annual reviews as I explained in Chapter 7. To do so, you will need a certificate from the mediation service and the local authority decision letter.

Why might I appeal after an annual review?

- There might be amendments that you disagree with.
- The LA might decide to cease the EHC plan (contrary to your wishes).
- The LA might decide not to make any changes (and you want them to).

Why haven't the local authority attended the annual review?
When local authorities have limited capacity, they prioritise the annual reviews where their input and presence is most needed. They may prioritise significant transition points, like phase transfer reviews, and requests for changes of placement or changes in funding. If your review is more standard and there actually aren't many changes being requested, then the LA might be less likely to attend.

What about if my child isn't in school?

Rebecca's son has an EHCP, but they have since withdrawn him from school because things were really not working. The EHCP is written for the school environment. It doesn't reflect their approach to learning at home. They can't replicate school at home and the provision and the needs just don't really relate to her son anymore. The EHCP is written for what he needs at school – what he does at home is different.

Rebecca doesn't like the EHCP. It describes her son's behaviour with derogatory words and is quite negative. She's had some assessments done privately which take a different approach, and her son has a diagnosis of autism with a PDA profile and ADHD. She now understands his experiences in the light of school trauma and EBSA (emotionally based school avoidance). The local authority have initiated the annual review process, but she's wondering if it's worth updating the EHCP as it all feels irrelevant to their current situation.

Rebecca has a plan and outcomes which are written for the school environment. She is not expected to work to those at home, and they no longer feel helpful. She is wondering if it's worth trying to get the EHCP updated and going through the annual review process.

If your child isn't attending school, the options available may depend on your local authority and your caseworker. It is a confusing area, as there is no clear guidance. There are two options. You can opt to try and have an EOTAS (education other than at school) package for them, or you can electively home educate. EOTAS packages are individually constructed and are bespoke to each child. They are decided through the EHCP process, and having this arrangement indicates that there is no suitable setting for your child. The local authority would still be financially involved in your child's education, for example funding an online tutor, or a regular morning at an animal farm. They would also have some oversight, through continued annual reviews. Children who are electively home educated do not receive any funding from the local authority. In both situations, parents often play a considerable role in managing their child's daily activities and provision.

ANNUAL REVIEWS AND TROUBLESHOOTING

It is worth considering what an EHCP will offer you, in your particular circumstances. If you're electively home educating, but your child had an EHCP when they were in school, the plan may continue unless you make a conscious choice to cease the plan. This means you will still have annual reviews and contact with the local authority. Some parents in this situation have a personal budget, or their child remains on roll with the school who provide some resources or tutoring.

SEN caseworkers may have a limited understanding of home education and are unlikely to have received any training in this area, so some parents find these interactions stressful. However, you might wish to retain contact with the system, to make returning to a setting easier should that be needed. Even if you do decide to cease your child's EHCP, the local authority is still legally obliged to provide an education for your child, should you decide you want your child to be in a setting again. You would however need to start the whole process of getting an assessment and a plan again from the beginning.

COFFEE TIME WITH ABI AND ELIZA

Eliza: Do they have to hold an annual review? Because we've had a few slip by and they haven't done it and I think that has come up when I've spoken to families that they're not always doing the annual reviews.

Abi: Legally, yes it's every year. I don't know what happens if it doesn't happen, but if they're in a setting, then the setting should be doing it.

Eliza: They should be doing it every year.

Abi: Yes.

Eliza: I would say probably with the annual review, just be mindful of when things are working, perhaps you have a new setting or something, try not to get too much of what's in the EHCP taken out. Just because it's working well right now doesn't mean it will always be working, and then you've lost the juicy bits. There's no harm in keeping bits in.

Abi: Annual reviews can be very stressful.

Eliza: You can feel like you're sort of going back to reliving difficult bits, can't it?

Abi: Yeah, exactly that. And it's quite a high stakes meeting, isn't it? Potentially. I remember talking to someone whose child was 18 or 20 and had complex needs. But every time he went to the annual review, the first thing they said was, so when are we going to end it? And he was initially a bit fazed by that, but he got used to it and got used to saying, we're not going to end it. He's going to have it until he's 25, which is the legal age up to when he can have it. But if he hadn't been prepared, then that would have knocked him off his feet. Or he might have not known an EHCP can go up to the age of 25.

Eliza: It seems like this post-16 setting is another time where you need to put your foot back on the pedal a little bit. Having been through it myself, but also talking to others who have, it's a time where local authorities will do a big push to get them back into the mainstream setting. So make sure that you've researched those settings and whether you feel that your child can do it.

CHAPTER 9

PARENTS' EXPERIENCES OF THE EHCP PROCESS

The EHCP process can be long and arduous. As I began to put this book together, I wondered if parents felt it was worth the fight at the end. I asked families to contact me with stories of their children being well supported, and I was overjoyed to be inundated with replies.

This chapter gives you a flavour of how it looks when things are going well – when school understands your child's needs, communicates well with you, and are flexible and able to accommodate difference. The children here are at a range of settings, both specialist and mainstream, and they are of different ages and have varying needs. There are however common threads in their stories, of outstanding home–school communication, a willingness in the staff to go the extra mile to support a child, a commitment to caring and nurturing children as individuals, and a willingness to think outside the box – to deconstruct it and rebuild it, to whatever shape it needs to be.

Here you will find the stories of:

- Tia, who goes to a mainstream secondary school
- Ashley, who is in a mainstream primary school
- Richard, who goes to a specialist secondary school
- Joe, who attends an autism resource unit in a secondary school
- Amir who is in a specialist secondary school
- Noah, who goes to a specialist school.

The first story is about Tia, who is in a mainstream secondary school. Jenny's daughter Tia's had a very difficult time in primary school. As she approached secondary school, the family were divided about whether mainstream or specialist provision would be best for her. They decided to try mainstream, and found a school where Tia has thrived and been seen as an individual. Jenny told me their story.

My daughter is now 12. From when she went to pre-school there were issues around social communication and sensory issues. As time went on, things got more difficult, not wanting to go to school, really challenging behaviour. School kept telling us that they couldn't do anything without a diagnosis. I said that is not how the law works. My understanding is that they should meet the needs of the child in front of them and not what a piece of paper says about them. But they were sticking with we need a diagnosis. We had the assessment done privately. Primary was traumatic for all of us. Her attainment was so poor that I wanted to withdraw her from SATS. She didn't meet the age-related expectations in all areas.

All of a sudden, COVID hit, and we had a lovely time at home. She was calm, she was regulated, we didn't have meltdowns, we didn't have any of it. We didn't do any of the formal learning they sent because that didn't work for her. We learned in other ways, we baked, we watched things grow, we planted things, and we talked about them. It was clear to me that this child if taught in the right way was capable of learning, but the school wasn't meeting her needs.

When she hit Year 5, her mental health deteriorated. We submitted the EHCP application. We went through the usual no, we're not going to assess. We went to mediation and at mediation I was told that the reason that they had decided not to assess was because there was no evidence from the school that she needed additional help. We sent everything off to the SEND tribunal. We agreed to a hearing on paper. I tried to work with school. I became a governor to try and change things from the inside. I did everything positive and proactive that you can do. It was now formal complaint time. The school got a new head, and then they submitted more information. The local authority decided to do the assessment – we didn't have a hearing.

That December the headteacher decided that the kids could wear their Christmas jumper for all of December. She came out on 1 December and said today was a really good day because I wasn't cold. I'm normally cold because I don't like the school jumper. It's seven years she has been wearing the school jumper. I'd asked for adjustments to her uniform constantly and been told no.

I wanted a specialist school but her dad really wanted her to stay in a mainstream school. The lady from the local authority said that based on what is in her plan, there would be no issue with specialist provision being provided for her. She said, 'Have a look at all these ones'. They were all quite a distance away and it would be a really long day, and Tia wouldn't have a social circle close by.

We decided to try mainstream with the plan in place. The plan really got her. The educational psychologist talked about staff taking an attitude of 'does it really matter?' Does it really matter if she's not doing homework, but she's in school and she's engaged and she's learning? Does it really matter if she's not attending every single lesson, but the ones that she does, she's making good progress in? Does it really matter if she's not in full school uniform?

She went to secondary and the SENCO was fab. She came to meet Tia in primary school and just straightaway got her. She started this new school last September. Honestly, I just don't know who the child in front of me is anymore. She has absolutely thrived. They've made it their mission to focus on inclusivity. They did a half term on neurodivergence and the things that some of us can cope with that others can't, and preferences and tastes and what some people like and other people don't. It has been amazing.

We walked into the maths classroom and the teaching assistant said to Tia 'I gather that you don't like maths very much and it's one of the big things that stress you out. This is what we're going to do. You might be in here sometimes with one of us sitting with you, or you might come to this room and we might do it as a small group'. I just thought, wow. You know enough about her to be able to say to her we know what your concerns and what your fears are and those are valid, and this is what we're gonna do about it. People get me, they understand, they know what I need and what I'm going to struggle with and what I'm not.

Tia made more progress over the course of Year 7 than she did all the way through primary school. Having the EHCP meant that they were all aware of her, and I would get phone calls from the office letting me know if she'd had a wobbly day, because that has a knock-on effect for what I can hope to achieve in the evenings at home. I need to build in some time to take her somewhere to run it off and decompress – in summer that's easy but if it's in the winter I need to find an activity that's going to help her. Home–school communication was so good and it was so important. We had the odd wobbly but they were so infrequent that we could manage it.

It has been such a positive experience. She's done all sorts this year. If there's an opportunity coming up, she gets offered it. She performed on stage in front of loads of people that she didn't know. It's been incredible to think where she was. For a child who did not ever want to go to school, didn't want to engage, every single morning now she's sat ready to go, ready to get to school, ready to learn.

It's a mainstream school. It really is the little things for her that make a huge difference. And they're willing to give her choices. She feels like she's got some control over those choices and the big decisions that are being made about her life. Where there are things that cause her stress, I encourage her first of all to go and speak to whoever she needs to speak to. Where it's a bigger thing, I'll send an email and say, we're a bit worried about this. What's the workaround? How can you work with us on that? That's always going to get you a positive response at this school.

Some of the parents who shared their stories with me for this book happened to be teachers and spoke of how their own experience teaching informed the choices they made for their children, as well as giving them the confidence to suggest things to school, and try things out for themselves. Leah told me about her son Ashley's experience in primary school and described his provision, which includes a range of activities designed to play to his strengths and help him regulate himself. Ashley has the condition FASD (foetal alcohol spectrum disorder). He also has a diagnosis of ADHD and attachment needs.

Ashley came to live with me when he was about 18 months. He has a diagnosis of FASD and ADHD. He was diagnosed at about three. He's got quite extreme versions of both. It's the hyperactivity and the lack of cause and effect thinking. He's done things like blend his finger with a stick blender because he just wanted to see what would happen. He's seven now, he has survived.

I got his EHCP ready for him to start school. I knew what he'd be facing when he started school. I think people have a tendency to fob you off and say, don't worry, school are used to this sort of thing. He wouldn't have survived in a standard classroom. I chose a school that was calm and quiet, it was good from a sensory perspective. I chose it because he'd be with the same 30 children from the beginning. They're not mixed around, so he'd make his friends in Reception and be with them all the way through primary school.

We had a multi-disciplinary assessment and an amazing paediatrician who specialises in neurodevelopmental stuff. We had a brilliant early years SENCO and a brilliant early years educational psychologist. He has attachment needs on top of his FASD and his ADHD.

We had to go through tribunal to get the EHCP. The educational psychologist suggested things like that he would benefit from Forest School and horse riding, but the local authority took them out of the EHCP. They changed forest school to sensory walks. They said if he's struggling, he can go into the school garden or take a sensory walk. We went to tribunal to get those things, and to get a full-time one-to-one. My local authority doesn't like giving full-time one-to-one, but we did get it. He has 32.5 hours, to include unstructured times. Now, he has a very tight EHCP. It has phrases like 'use unconditional positive regard' because he struggles with even a grumpy face and being told off is very hard for him. He has horse riding one day a week and forest school one day, so it's less time in the classroom.

The school fought for more funding for him. He's been very lucky this year because he's got the same teacher and teaching assistants again so that's helped. There's a mismatch between the academic side and his peers. He's good at things like swimming and football. He takes lots of breaks, they go off and clean the pond out or dig potatoes. They meet his needs really well for a mainstream school. We have ups and downs, they make mistakes but I try and be really understanding about all that because it's the key stuff that is important. We did have a SENCO who wanted to make him more independent; she thought he should have less one-to-one time. But the whole thing of FASD is that the needs don't go away – even into adulthood, he's always going to need a high level of supervision.

Children with FASD often have a spiky profile where their

expressive language is better than their understanding. It depends on his sensory overwhelm – if he's overwhelmed, you're literally speaking to him like a dog, 'Ashley, stop now' it's like three words. But if he's calm and in a good place, then you can have a good chat with him. He has to be really settled for his language processing to work. He has two teaching assistants.

Relationships are key for him. Somebody who understands what's going on and can interpret his intentions, but also help him to understand. He's very chatty, and he'll go and chat to all the neighbours. He loves all the staff at school, and he likes that social side. He's more influenced by peers, so perhaps if he was surrounded by others with high special needs he'd be learning behaviours. He's vulnerable with his peers. I see him on play dates and he's a scapegoat. If something's going wrong, they can blame him, and everyone will assume it is him. He will do anything to please his friends.

He doesn't like writing or reading, so he throws his books and things. He can't read yet and he's seven. I've given up on phonics because it just isn't working for him. He can segment, he can blend, he can do all the components, but he can't put it all together and read. Apparently it's easier for children with FASD to learn by the old 'look and say' method. I've bought a set of Peter and Jane books and we started them in the holidays. I took them into school and his teacher was very happy to take that on board and they're his school reading books now. They do listen to me as well, which I think helps. I've done a parenting for children with FASD course which gives me the confidence to identify things.

He gets a taxi to school as well, and that really helps my own stress levels. He goes into breakfast club for about ten minutes so that he gets into his classroom before all the rest of the children so that he isn't going into a busy classroom. He goes in first and then the noise and everything builds up. He also goes home first before all the kind of hustle and bustle of everyone leaving.

PARENTS' EXPERIENCES OF THE EHCP PROCESS

The story that follows was told to me by Meg, who is the mother of Richard. Richard managed primary school, but the demands of the secondary school environment meant he started refusing to go. After a period out of education, he now attends a specialist setting.

> My son seemed to get along fine in primary school. He was always considered quiet, but there were no problems, he attended great. First week into secondary school, the problems started where he just wasn't coping with the environment. We approached the head of year, tried to get some help. They were a bit hesitant because it's mainstream. They don't want to change too much because then they've got to try and change things for everybody else. Then he just started refusing to go to school – he couldn't cope. We kept getting threats of, you're gonna get fined if he doesn't come in. Doesn't matter if he's kicking and screaming, doesn't matter if he's upset, we just need him in school. I said I'm not

doing that, it's traumatic, I can see he doesn't want to be there, and he's not a naughty child, he's not doing it for those kind of reasons.

They contacted Children's Services, as a threat to us. Children's Services said it doesn't seem like that school is right for him. They wrote us a letter of support to get an EHCP. The school had said we couldn't get one. We put in the application, and it was approved straightaway. I was quite shocked. I was waiting for a fight.

We saw the educational psychologist who understood my son really well, but they did name the mainstream secondary that he hadn't attended for months. We went to mediation, it went to panel, and then they decided to put him in the specialist school. He started there in January, and they put him in the 'nurturing club', is what they call it. It was a class of just one other child at the time, and my son. It's just getting them used to being in a school, they can do whatever they want whilst they're there. They don't have to wear school uniform. They don't have to eat there if they don't feel comfortable.

The class he's in now has only five other children, it's not a full class. There's one teacher, and one mental health support teacher. They have lessons, but they don't have to do them if they don't want to. It's all very calm, they don't have to do PE if they don't want to, they don't have to get changed if they don't want to, they have break time and lunchtime, but again, you don't have to go up for that if you don't want to. There are no loud bells to tell you that your lesson's ending. It's very much like primary school in a sense of you're in your class and that's where you are all day.

A lot of people are put off applying for an EHCP because they think 'I'm not going to get it, I'm going to have this huge battle', but I think you just need to go for it. You just need to try. I mean, you know your child, so if you think that's what they need, then absolutely.

Michelle's son Amir had an EHCP from when he was young, but it was hard to find the right place for him. When they did find a nurturing setting where they had trust in the staff, it was a massive relief for the whole family, and he has thrived.

> When Amir was two the nurse said to us, do you know your child's not quite like other children? We went through speech and language and we went through early help. We had some parenting courses. Even before he went to school, we went to panel because professionals were saying that these needs seem to be quite high.
>
> He wasn't communicating the way others do and he was getting frustrated and angry. They said mainstream will meet his needs but almost immediately it went downhill and he became very distressed. He would do anything he could to

get out, so he became violent. He got an ASD diagnosis aged six. The LA don't use the term PDA but it was very clear to us.

We got an EHCP in place and he went to a supported unit, but it was still too busy, even the echoing off the corridor walls was driving him nuts. He went to another unit with higher needs, but again, we were being called into meetings. He attacked people, he would do anything to get out. Halfway through Year 4, we had an emergency annual review meeting and the school said he needs a specialist SEMH (social, emotional, and mental health) setting.

We went to look and there was a boy smashing one of the windows. He was inside, he had a chair, but he also had gloves on and goggles on. The teacher said, I know that looks horrific, but he's safe. There's an adult at the end of the room. And he's going to be allowed to get all of those feelings out. And then tomorrow, he'll probably help us fix it. And both me and my husband immediately relaxed. Here was a place where children could be themselves and let the adults know exactly how they felt, however they wanted to, and then they'd be shown how to make amends for that and then worked with to improve things.

He started there in Year 5. Each teacher has the class for two years, so there's less transitioning. They select the kids in the class to be as compatible as they can. If you've got a very active group, they're put together; or a very quiet, sensitive group, they're put together – rather than grouping by ability, because with the small holistic approach that they've got, they can tailor the curriculum and differentiate it within the classroom. The kids are still getting what they need academically, but they're matched much more closely to an environment that will suit them. He said I'm allergic to writing, don't make me do it. The teacher said we're going to leave him alone until he's over his allergy.

He thrived. They were so brilliant. They'd phone us up and they'd say, 'What did we do wrong? Why is he upset today? What do you think it is?' They set up all these new PDA-friendly techniques where the kids could just filter in, and their stations would be set up, but there was no come and sit down at your table. They sit where they want. They sit on the floor. They get out what they want and we'll start teaching and they'll join us when they want to. They might not always get things right, but they always listen to you. And that is what's really working, the communication.

He's meeting far more goals now. They have a built-in sensory diet and a holistic therapeutic way of doing it. They do the thrive approach. They have a forest school and lots of art outreach, music outreach. They gain confidence in everything they do, and they have these small introductions to new sensations and new activities with no expectation of having to achieve anything. It's all just about doing. There's no goal at the end of it, other than to let them get in there and build up their confidence.

The teacher said, 'I love sleepovers, don't you?' All the class said, 'We've never been invited to a sleepover'. She arranged a sleepover at school and they took their teddies and their sleeping bags and they had campfires and marshmallows and a movie. This is the only time my son's been to a sleepover, but he remembers it.

There is a trust that they can deliver what he needs. We have that with them all the time. We know we can trust them with him. It's a small school, every single lad in that school, the staff know what they love. They can tell when they're upset before they've opened their mouths. When you visit for a parent's evening or sports day, you can tell the love for each person in there and it really makes a difference.

They really support us as families. You'll be lining up to log in and they'll go 'How's your new job? How's the baby?' They know what's going on with us, and they offer family

> support. They will link you up with local charities, mental health support, they signpost you. You really feel like they know all of you so that you're believed when you say there's a problem, you're believed. And when they say things are fine, you believe them because they know what's going on in there.
>
> They build in early communication. It's not just a piece of paper that they look at once a year. Now he's in Year 10, they do a two-day-a-week outreach to the local college, so they'll have technical skills and vocational skills, and then they spend some time concentrating on doing some GCSEs, which we never thought he'd do. That gives him a two-year run-up to leave there, so they're preparing them early.
>
> Because it's a social and emotional specialist setting, they really teach them to tell their feelings and their experience, but support each other as well. When you're in a bad place, you lose hope. But this is the kind of thing you can expect actually, and people can do it and they deserve it and it's there.

Joe found school more difficult than other children from the beginning. His parents sought help from lots of different teams and professionals, and he received a diagnosis of autism and ADHD. By the end of primary school he wasn't attending any lessons, but transitioned successfully to a secondary school with a specialist resource base, which he loves. His mother, Flick, spoke to me about their experience.

> It became clear from within six to eight months of starting school that Joe was finding life more difficult than the average, but he managed okay in Reception. When he went into Year 1, he was struggling with the structure and the rigidity, and needing to sit down a lot of the time. In school he was difficult to manage. He'd have lots of tantrums, refusing to do what he was told. He'd walk out of the room, he'd kick the

chair or throw the chair over as he walked out. By the end of Year 2, we were being called in on an almost daily basis. He had various reward chart systems, but nothing consistent that worked for him. He was deteriorating in terms of his happiness, and his engagement with learning. He was viewed by the school as emotionally immature and not managing rather than anything else. We were wondering if he was neurodiverse. He was having lots more meltdowns at home. In retrospect, I think I'd probably been doing quite a lot of things at home to help him manage it without realising.

We moved him into the independent sector when he was in Year 3. They said we think he might be autistic. COVID hit about two weeks later and Joe had to go to key worker school, which was just a disaster for him because there was no routine. I was called repeatedly to pick him up because he'd become very aggressive and violent and just be doing everything he possibly could to get out of there. He was referred for NHS autism assessment, which was declined. We went back into the state sector.

We spent a lot more time thinking about what was gonna be the right place for him. We went for a village primary with just a single class per year. We were quite open with the head that we thought he was going to need an EHCP and that he needed to be referred and assessed for autism. We paid for a private autism assessment because the school were applying for an EHCP and the more evidence we had the better in terms of support for him.

He struggled with any form of change, anything at all. If there was a different teacher, anything in the day that was different, different seating, anything that was noisy, lunchtimes, people shouting, he really struggled in the unstructured lessons. Things like PE and drama, he just couldn't manage to get on with people. He spent more and more time inside, because he found the playground too noisy, and he developed this fear of balls. Anytime any ball came anywhere near him, he would be running off screaming.

When he was five or six, his behaviours were not completely in line with some of his peers. By the time he was eight or nine, it was clear that his meltdowns and the things he was finding difficult were out of the normal range and his ability to communicate with his peers in a normal way wasn't there. He's got very particular interests. He would just talk at people about what he was interested in and wouldn't listen to their responses at all. He struggled more with friendships and became more isolated. He became more aggressive in school. If he was upset about something, he would hurl all the books off the shelves. He would chuck chairs across the room. Anything that another child did to him that was an accident, he would deem a slight against him and an intentional misdemeanour. Someone would accidentally knock him with a bag and he'd turn around and wallop them because in his view they'd purposely knocked into him aiming to hurt him.

In Year 2 we saw a clinical psychologist because we wanted some strategies to help manage his behaviour. He also had some EMDR around processing change, and all the changes through COVID. We had those things to go on his EHCP and then we went for a private diagnosis of autism as well.

Our head was really proactive. They got the local authority autism team in to assess him, before the EHCP. The teacher who saw him was just a teacher who specialised in that, and wrote a report that also went in the EHCP, and then they did some sessions with staff to look at what might help him in terms of regulation and managing him. The staff were able to access some restraint training. It was three months spent gathering as much information about him as possible. We were advised to do a parenting course, which we did.

Having it all together there with the first application definitely makes a difference, as well as having it from lots of different sources saying the same thing. We had four or five different reports all saying the same issue and the same needs. We had it from the clinical psychologist, the EMDR therapist, and the local authority SEND team. The LA educational psychologist then said the same as well. Their educational psychologist watched him for a couple of hours and did a discussion with us, and with the school. It was very clear what support was needed. It was granted at 20 weeks with no appeals. It was helpful in some ways. He got funding for a one-to-one teaching assistant for 80% of the time.

After the EHCP, when he turned ten, he was referred for ADHD and started medication as well. The school really struggled to employ a teaching assistant with any SEND experience. He became more disengaged and isolated, and went on a reduced timetable in the first term of Year 6. The EHCP definitely helped us there because having that already in place meant that the local authority were really quick with their alternative provision. He had alternative provision within about six weeks. We, together with school said to the local authority that we didn't feel the school could meet his needs at that time. He was in school for 50% of the time, and he had alternative provision for 50% of the time. He had two half days of forest school. He did a session with horse riding for the disabled and he had a science tutor, because he loves science, and we paid for a therapist. We really felt school couldn't meet his needs and I felt he needed specialist provision. The local authority were keen to get him through Year 6 and then look at the options that we had for secondary.

His EHCP unlocked the door to the autism resource unit of a local secondary. You had to have an autism diagnosis and an EHCP. We knew he wouldn't manage in mainstream, but he's a bright child. We wanted him to have the opportunity to do a range of GCSEs, not just a few. A lot of the specialist provision has quite limited access. His statutory assessment key worker was really helpful. We spent a lot of time looking at options for him and what would suit him best.

It's been an absolute game changer for him. By the end of Year 6, he wasn't in any of his lessons. Now, going into Year 8, he has 80–85% lesson attendance. He's a much happier child. He likes school. The care he gets there is phenomenal. They understand what autistic ADHD kids need. It's very individualised. They think, 'What do we need to do to enable this child to access education?'

He does emotional regulation sessions. He does English catch-up sessions and he does gardening. They're proactively working on his emotional regulation. You can see the change in the year. Even now he deals with situations that a year ago he would have just flipped out. He's much more able to walk away and not see the slights in everything that happens in school.

He now goes to a specialist unit which is part of a big state secondary. Joe goes there at 8 o'clock in the morning, he settles in there, and then he gets taken to his first lesson at 8.30 am. He has a subject-specific TA for each one of his subjects who takes him to the lesson. He leaves his lessons five minutes early so he can go through the corridors when it's quiet and get into the next lesson and is handed over to the next TA. He has some subjects which he finds easier from an attention point of view and some that he finds more frustrating. The ones that are more frustrating he does 30 minutes in the lesson and 20 minutes outside. He still has to complete the work, but he can do that work in the library. If he's feeling really fizzy in a lesson, one of the TAs can take him out and they've got equipment where he can just burn off some energy or quietly read a book. The aim is that he's in the mainstream school lessons at least 80% and then the unit when he needs to be. He spends his break and his lunch in the unit. There's usually some form of activity going on there in the year groups to build friendships, but they're also really good at finding a corner. They're very good at targeting him to go and sit down and do something to help regulate. They also do social circuits and social skills once a week. They work on teamwork, sharing group activities, and peer relations. He has his pictorial timetable up on the board, so that he knows what's happening all the time.

He has a group of regular TAs who sit in with him all the time. Their aim between Year 7 and Year 11 is to gradually reduce the need to have a TA all the time. Different children move at different rates and they work with that. We opt him out of all homework apart from maths and science and all tests apart from maths and science. He started the year doing all the tests, and he was getting more and more anxious because it was like a test a week.

Joe really likes Minecraft. One of the science teachers has agreed to set up a Minecraft club, specifically because Joe and another child have that interest, to try and get them in. The school bell was chosen by the kids in the unit. It's not a bell, it's a much duller drone.

One of his lessons is religion, philosophy, and ethics, and they don't have their own classrooms for that. They have that lesson in whatever classroom is free. Joe's had been in the maths classroom for the year, and he just could not go with it. We can't have this lesson, which is all about non-factual things, in a classroom that's a fact classroom. I can't do that lesson in that classroom, it's wrong. I was astonished when the head came up to me and said, 'We can look at moving the classroom. Nobody else in the classroom cares which room it is in. The teacher doesn't care what room it is in. Therefore, if there is another room available at the same time, that isn't a maths classroom, why wouldn't we try?' I was just blown away.

He's a child who wants to go to school and we spent years fighting him into the car and through the door of primary school. It's really nice to see him enjoying learning, enjoying education, and feeling positive about his future. He loves learning, he loves facts, he loves knowledge. He just couldn't manage in that environment as it was.

> When you suddenly have a child that isn't going to school, it's really difficult to work out what's the right thing to do. How hard do you push for things? What options do you have? It's a minefield practically and emotionally, managing constantly with a child who's very dysregulated and very unhappy in a place they have to go most of the time.
>
>
>
> I'm still grateful for the fact that when I go and pick him up, I don't have a sense of apprehension. For many years, I had a real feeling of apprehension every time I went to pick him up because it would always be, 'Joe has done this, Joe has done that'. School deal with what happens in school. They will sort it out and they'll tell us what happened, but it's very much, 'This is what happened. This is what's been sorted and this is where we are'. There is nothing of the anxiety and apprehension that was there for a long time.

The final story in this chapter is told by Nicole. Her son, Noah, has a rare chromosomal disorder. He has speech and language problems and has support from a multi-disciplinary team. He went to his local primary first, and is now thriving in a specialist provision.

Our son Noah was born with a rare chromosomal disorder. Having a diagnosis early helped us in terms of being able to access provision going into school. We already had a lot of professionals involved because he's needed speech and language, OT, and physio all from the get go. He already had a good team with a lot of information. He did start in a mainstream primary school, but his speech and language problems were quite complex. He's nearly nine and his language is more like a four-year-old, so very repetitive, and clarity of speech is quite difficult. He also needed a structured regime of physio, and he needed sensory OT, in school provision. Our local primary was okay to start, but we knew he would need to go to specialist provision at some point. He needs lots of personal care; he's still in nappies and so on – towards the end it got quite difficult in mainstream to be able to manage that.

The school tended to keep children with special needs behind, and we wanted him to stay with his peers, but have a relevant curriculum. We started the EHCP process, and 18 months down the line we had a place for him. He's really thrived. We can see so much progress. It's small steps compared to our other children, and it looks very different, but school are really positive. They're ambitious. And there's a real drive to make sure they get the best out of life they can. It's all about how can we set them up to be as independent as possible.

They've got a full accessible sensory room. They've got rebound therapy, trampoline, soft play, hydropool. They have separate health care, separate feeding teams, and separate personal care teams so the teachers and the staff in the class are not taken out to do that stuff. They have all the people that they need to look after them without taking away from the actual in-class stuff. I think that makes a massive difference because they don't have to stop to take them out.

They really encourage not having one-to-one – it's more

one-to-three, so that they're not just, this is my person and that's it. They stream their children in terms of need, so my son is in the complex communication needs stream, then they've got different pathways tailored to the children's individual needs. He spent three years in one class. The curriculum is really specific. They're really good at personalising it so he knows this is the bit he's got to do. Sometimes it's with other people, sometimes it's on his own. It's a good mix of supported and independent, you know, letting him have a go. It's not all structured. They do let them investigate. It's like EYFS/Key Stage 1.

He was under 14 different consultants when we applied for it. From gastro to his eyes, speech and language, a dietician, he has a full range. He's got ARFID as well as sensory difficulties and his global delay diagnosis and we're under the autism pathway. They say he's got autistic traits, but they're not defining the diagnosis because he already has a diagnosis. They're waiting developmentally to see whether or not it does fit further down the line.

It took us 18 months to get the EHCP and the school place. We started as soon as he went into school nursery. They rejected the request straightaway so we appealed. We ended up going through mediation and the school said we can meet his needs. We ended up almost at tribunal about it. We had the data from nursery and school to show the progress he'd made in two years was quite negligible. They conceded the day the evidence pack needed to be in. Then the first plan came out and they wouldn't name a school because they weren't going to name the special school. We had to appeal that, and wait a bit longer. They send special transport, and they've got chaperones. I worried about it, but actually it's his favourite part.

Our SENDIAS were not very good at all. They told us, if they reject it, you'll not get an EHCP and you won't get a special school. She was very much down the LA line, graduated approach, it'll be fine with quality first teaching. We went to IPSEA (Independent Provider of Special Education Advice). I did the SEND Level 1 course, and we wrote our own letter to the head of the children's services at the LA.

Our LA believe their system is entirely inclusive and that mainstream school is the perfect place for any child with special needs. Because he was in nursery, they didn't believe that he would need a spot. I've worked with children that are two years into it and still not any further forwards. I always tell parents, keep going. SENCOs are told they need a certain amount of funding or they need a certain amount of assessment cycles to apply. I say go and read the SEN Code of Practice and I quote it to them.

Our area is notorious for early knockbacks and the first application being rejected no matter what. We were prepared but still very surprised. Mediation was a waste of time. My husband did the mediation meeting and he ended up really frustrated. School were trying to make themselves look like they were a good school helping this child, and didn't want to be seen as failing. But at the same time, they had told us something totally different and we knew from the data that it was totally different. They said it's all been

> good, we can keep him where he is. We ended up at tribunal because we felt that the mediation had actually done nothing to help us as a family or us as parents to get him what he needed. It felt like they were just doing lip service to it and not letting it be effective in any way.

AND FINALLY...

Eliza: I feel like the provision that we found was the last part of the healing process. They made me feel that we weren't a failure, that there was something that could work out there. There are things out there that can work and it feels good to find that. You don't have to do it on your own and you're not the only one who gets your child. There's no reason you should have to do it all.

I was reminded of that recently because I forgot how much of that they carry for me. Her being able to go somewhere is just amazing. Someone taking a bit of that, because I'm a full-time parent, someone doing a bit of it for me, and I trust them to do that.

Abi: Someone else caring about them, and how they are, right? I remember really feeling that when I found a nursery I liked. I was like, phew, someone else loves him. They really care about him, they are doing their best for him, it's not all on me.

Eliza: It's funny, isn't it? You say that about love. I suppose people would be hesitant to use that, but my boyfriend said that when we went to look at her college, this specialist college provision, he went, they really love her, don't they? And I said, yeah, that's what I feel there. It's a real care. And I feel the care for the parent as well.

Abi: Yes, I felt that at the nursery too – they ask how I am. Sometimes they are the only person who does that all day.

Eliza: She used to send me emails going, this didn't work, but we're trying something else. It's part of the healing process and recovery for us. Things can work, things can go well.

For some parents, they're burnt out, and the child's burnt out. They want to deregister and just not do it. And that's fine, you can always access this system again, if you want to, or if you feel ready. But also for others like myself, I know that it would have felt like I had lost that safety net. To me it felt like a recognition of need and I needed that.

Abi: I've never really thought about it like that. You're saying that even if you're not in a setting, it is a layer of support and recognition.

Eliza: It means different things to different people. If you are home educating, it can be a recognition of how hard it is. It brings some clarity.

Abi: I think for everyone, it's different what it is and why you need it or want it. I really love the cartoons you've drawn for this final chapter. They bring to life such great stories of staff really going the extra mile, and caring so much about the children in their care. Putting them first, and adapting what they are doing to make it work.

Eliza: Finding somewhere where they're happy to go, that's all we want. It can seem really hard. But you can find things that work. This lays the stepping stones to allow them to become an adult who can do more. It's a long-term game.

FUTURE

References

Autism Education Trust. (n.d.). *What is autism?* www.autismeducationtrust.org.uk/about/what-is-autism

Department for Education (DfE) and Department of Health (DoH). (2015). *Special educational needs and disability code of practice: 0 to 25 years.* www.gov.uk/government/publications/send-code-of-practice-0-to-25

Department for Education (DfE). (2025). *Special educational needs in England.* https://explore-education-statistics.service.gov.uk/find-statistics/special-educational-needs-in-england/2024-25

Jemal, J., & Kenley, K. (2023). Wasting money, wasting potential: The cost of SEND tribunals. *PBE.* https://pbe.co.uk/publications/wasting-money-wasting-potential-the-cost-of-send-tribunals

Long, R., & Roberts, N. (2025). *Special needs support in England, research briefing 07020.* House of Commons Library. https://researchbriefings.files.parliament.uk/documents/SN07020/SN07020.pdf

Useful organisations

- My Child Is Not Fine at School (Facebook group)
- IPSEA
- SEN Jungle
- SOS SEN
- Your local SENDIAS